Take Two Aspirin....

The Escapades of a
Royal Air Force Medic.

Brian Dixon

First published in Great Britain in 2008

Copyright © Brian Dixon, 2008

ISBN 978-0-9558513-0-8

A CIP catalogue record for this book is
available from the British Library

All photographs © Brian Dixon 2008
Cover photograph © Mark Dixon 2008

Dedicated to Pauline and Mark
for their love and support.

To my family for their love and encouragement.

In memory of those I knew,
who gave their life in the service of their country.

R.I.P.
Jon, Rick, Graham, Kevin, Mick, Bob, Steve, Vince, Dave.

Introduction

This book was originally written with the intention of supporting my family history research. However, it evolved into the publication you see before you now. It has been written as accurately as memories and dusty documents allow so, if you recognise yourself and the story is not as you recall, it's too bad because I don't intend to re-write everything again!

The names of everyone on these pages have been changed, apart from my immediate family and those with whom I served who gave their life in the service of their country. Those names, in particular, should never be forgotten.

It was written over a number of months and gave me many happy memories of my time in the Royal Air Force. I hope it gives you some of that pleasure too, as you re-take that twelve year journey with me.

Brian Dixon

Chapter 1

Ever since I can remember, I wanted to join the Royal Air Force. Now, here I was, sitting on the rear ramp of a Chinook helicopter, flying over London, in the post Gulf War victory fly-past celebration. It was a cold and misty morning, but I didn't feel anything other than immense pride to have been associated with something as historic as the Persian Gulf War in 1991.

Not only that, but I was at what I considered to be the top of my tree, in the elite Royal Air Force's own Special Forces Flight. I was their medic. The only medic that they had ever had. Even though they had been in operation some ten years. As I was to find out, I was to be the only medic that had served with them on a regular basis, at that time.

My interest in flying has been with me for as long as I can remember. All I ever wanted to do when I left school was to fly in the Royal Air Force. However, I didn't want to be one of those fast jet jockeys, zooming around the sky at Mach 1, seeing everything as a split second blur. I wanted to be a helicopter pilot. The versatility of those wondrous beasts applied to my sense of adventure. I could imagine myself piloting a big yellow rescue helicopter, hovering over some poor soul, their very existence dependent upon my ability to skilfully guide my aircraft into a position whereupon a rescue could be effected. If not a search and rescue helicopter, a military helicopter of any form would do. I suppose it was the thought of flying at a slower pace, enjoying the sensation of flight, and the sheer exhilaration of being in control in a three dimensional world, by right a world only available to birds, that was to be my desire for all my boyhood years. Unfortunately, a desire that would go unfulfilled.

Prior to turning the age of thirteen, I satisfied my craving for all things concerning flying with collecting magazines, chocolate bar aviation offers and building hundreds of Airfix models. My bedroom ceiling had numerous dogfights taking place. Spitfires were taking on Saab Viggens, and Messershmits were fighting Lysanders and Sopwith Camels. Unfortunately, there were not very many models of helicopters to be found. All of these things cost money. I never knew how little spare cash there was to go around. As with most children of our age, my brother and I were oblivious to the sacrifices made by our parents so that we could have our hobbies and little extras. Often, the Sunday roast would be sausage casserole or other such treat (I still enjoy sausage, mash and gravy). I don't suppose I ever said thank you, but I will always be eternally grateful for the unselfish sacrifices that my parents made.

At the ripe old age of thirteen I took my first steps towards realising my dream and joined the local Air Training Corps. It was 1966 Squadron, based in the playing fields in Wavetree, Liverpool. After a period of settling in, I was eventually issued a uniform. Now, I wasn't the world's most normal sized individual. Tall and very skinny was the order of the day. We were issued the old "hairy Mary" style of uniform – battle dress and trousers, dark blue shirts, black tie and beret. I rapidly came to the conclusion that there were no tall, very skinny people in the RAF. I looked like a small child off to a fancy dress party, with a beret like a helicopter landing pad! However, apart from the itchiness of the material, I was happy to wear my uniform. Eventually, my older brother, Alec, joined as a cadet followed by my Dad as a civilian instructor. It must have been so peaceful for my Mum every Tuesday and Friday evening. Subjects were many and varied. Drill, first aid, airmanship and Morse code, to name but a few. They even let us play with real rifles! I remember one day going off to an open air rifle range to fire the old fashioned Lee Enfield .303 bolt action rifle. It had a kick like a mule. We all placed our folded up berets on our right shoulder to act as a pad. Assuming the position, and fighting against the heavy weight of the rifle, I gently squeezed the trigger. Next thing I recall was the loudest bang I had ever heard, even with ear defenders on. There was a simultaneous big kick into my shoulder. I moved back down the range about an inch or two, without even getting to my feet. I was so skinny it would not have surprised me to have pulled the trigger, shot backwards and just have the bullet stay still and fall to the floor! Anyway, the bang and kick to the shoulder was immediately followed by the pain of having my beret badge embedded into my shoulder. Guess who hadn't padded that bit. After firing off the ten rounds in the magazine, I was relieved to be able to stand up, even if it was some six inches further back from where I started. My arms were aching, my shoulder was throbbing, my ears were pounding and my elbows and knees were red from the backward thrust of my body. What a way to spend an evening.

I stayed in the cadets for over three years, leaving only to join the RAF. At one stage, I transferred to 1988 Squadron in Huyton. I was lucky enough to attend two summer camps – one at RAF Manston and the other at RAF Odiham; as it happened, the station, which would be my last and most enjoyed. On July 19th 1977, I had my first flight with the RAF. It was whilst on summer camp at Manston. The aircraft was the good old faithful Chipmunk, the Skoda of the RAF fleet. Trusted only to pilots over the age of 90 and to cadets who knew no different. I thoroughly enjoyed the 30-minute flight though. Later, the same day, I took a flight in a Mk 2 Wessex of 22Sqn. I was in seventh heaven. Well, for thirty minutes, anyway. Apart from my first helicopter flight, the highlight of that camp was getting into trouble and having to re-varnish the Hurricane gate guard. Being given authority to climb and crawl over one of the finest designed aircraft of all time, flown only by heroes, was my idea of punishment! I imagined what was going through the pilot's mind prior to taking off and facing the enemy and I wanted some of that romantic glamour. The following year, summer camp was at RAF Odiham. I was fortunate enough to have two flights in helicopters. On July 17th 1978, (almost a year to the day of my first flight), in a Wessex Mk 2, and again on 21 July 1978 in a Puma of 33Sqn. Helicopter flying was definitely for me! To those who have never been fortunate enough to fly in a helicopter, there is little point in trying to explain the experience. It is nothing like fixed wing flying. I still have the cadet group photograph taken at RAF Odiham, standing by the

Whirlwind helicopter gate guard, which stands outside of the medical centre where I was due to return some twelve years later.

Whilst in the cadets, I also had the opportunity to go gliding. This was at RAF Burtonwood, an old Second World War American Air Force Base, sadly in decline. The main runway now formed a stretch of the M62 motorway. The only American presence was in the large storage depot, which was rumoured to have several underground levels in which secret military hardware was stored. I never did find out whether there was any truth in those rumours, but the Americans I saw were often quite twitchy and protective of their property. Gliding was very enjoyable. It was another different form of flying. However, for me, it was no substitute for the thrill of rotary wing flying. First thing you do after climbing in the cockpit of the Kirkby Cadet Mk3 glider, is religiously go through the checklist: Controls – rotate the stick to make sure that it had full, unrestricted movement; Ballast – weight of both the pilot and passenger, ensuring they were both within safety parameters (occasionally, extra weights were added to the front in the case of lightweights like me); Straps – tight and locked; Instruments – glass in tact, altimeter set to zero and barometric pressure correctly entered; Trim – set to a central position; Canopy – not fitted on the gliders we were using; Brakes – air brakes were not fitted, but we had a braking mechanism called a spoiler which disrupted the airflow over the top of the wing, thereby giving us the aerodynamics of a housebrick. The whole check was commonly referred to as CB-SIT-CB. Over a period of time, the pre-flight checks became second nature. This was great as I saw it as the first step to flying with the RAF. The aim was to get me to a proficient state so that I could fly the glider solo. I did eventually manage it but there were some interesting moments on the way! RAF Burtonwood, as I have already mentioned, ran along the edge of the M62 motorway. Next to us was the motorway service station, which looked like a pair of Red Indian Tepees, one on either side of the motorway. Also nearby was a line of high power electricity cables, complete with pylons. To cap it off, RAF Burtonwood was one of the few Air Cadet gliding schools, which took off and landed on a concrete runway. I was reminded of the landing surface on more than one occasion! Many silly things used to happen when at 635 Gliding School. I once remember a launch cable breaking, during a launch, and rather than land on the busy motorway, the pilot decided to try to fly the glider around a tight turn to get back onto the airfield. Hanging from underneath the glider was a broken length of launch cable. As the pilot managed to face the airfield, safety being paramount, he decided to pull the release toggle to get rid of the cable, prior to landing. After releasing the cable, the small parachute on the end, which is designed to prevent the cable plummeting to earth, inflated. We all watched as it slowly drifted towards the electricity cables, and cheered and applauded loudly at the big blue flash and loud bang that followed. The local population was not over pleased with us as it took about eight hours for the electricity board to sort the problem out!

I was lucky enough to continue my glider pilot training and foolishly, my instructor, Alfie Lewis, decided that I had done enough to be allowed to take one of the gliders into the air on my own. On 18 May 1980, following a couple of check flights from the Chief Instructor, Pilot Officer Leggett, I was finally given the go-ahead to fly solo. I remember Pilot Officer Leggett getting out of the seat behind me and giving me the pep talk of, "Just go up, around and down for your first one" as he was fastening down the straps to the now empty seat. "OK, This is it" I thought to myself. "My first flight of a long and illustrious aviation career." I looked down at the concrete of the runway. "Wings level" I shouted, trying to hide the mixture of nerves and sheer delight. A cadet colleague picked up the wing off the ground and held the glider in a level attitude. "Fix cable!" Another cadet attached the cable to the front of the glider, out of my field of vision, near the bottom left area at the front of the cockpit. I felt the tug, testing that the cable was securely attached. "All clear above and behind!" The cadet on the wingtip looked in the direction required and repeated, "All clear above and behind". In actual fact, there was nothing allowed anywhere near us, especially when there was a first solo about to launch. "Take up slack!" The thin wire cable slowly snaked along the ground until, with a jerk, the glider nudged forward and the cable stretched in a perfectly straight line down the runway. This was it, I thought. A momentous event about to take place. "All out!" This was the command to begin the launch. A signaller changed the light signals from slow flashes (take up slack) to fast flashes (all out). The winch operator saw the change, and increased the speed in which the cable was rewound on the large wooden drums. The glider began to accelerate and the cadet on the wing began running, in order to keep up with me. I continued to accelerate until the wingman could no longer keep up and he released the wing. I was now truly on my own.

Keep an eye on the airspeed. Once it reaches the predetermined speed, pull back on the stick and, hey presto, the glider starts to rise. Keep it level, keep the airspeed on, watch the height. If anything happens now, this is the most critical time. RAF Burtonwood is a very unforgiving environment. There is truly very little room to take avoiding action. Never mind. I'm now approaching 1000 feet. Time to slightly lower the nose and take the tension off the cable and ensure that there will be sufficient airspeed. I pull the yellow toggle three times to make sure that the cable has released and feel the catapulting effect as I am thrown clear. One thousand feet below me I can see the yellow winch that has just assisted me into the air. I am astonished by the silence of it all, as there is no instructor shouting at me. My emotions are in overdrive and completely mixed. There is absolute delight that I have finally managed to fly solo. There really is no one else up here with me. I fight the fear that if something does go wrong, then it will be up to me to sort it out. If I don't, then the consequences will almost certainly be final. The joy of flight and the sense of achievement are superb. With all this going on, I am still concentrating on the flying. If I do a good job, I may be invited to stay on as a staff cadet and progress further. The view is, as usual, spectacular. The motorway stretches in both directions, with a wigwam on either side. The runway is where it should be. I note the windsock and decide where to make my crosswind turn before, again turning, to run parallel with the runway. At the chosen point I turn crosswind again, this time to land, before finally turning into the wind to make the approach for landing. Thankfully all went well during the flight and I start to go through the landing sequence. Check height and speed. Open the spoilers to reduce lift. Line up on the runway and again check speed. Prior to landing, at a height of about fifty feet, I closed the spoilers and raised the nose of the glider to reduce the airspeed further. Above the runway now, airspeed dropping off, I gently fall until I feel the now familiar bump of returning to terra firma. Opening the spoilers again, to make sure I don't leap frog down the runway. I somehow manage to get the glider down and keep it down, before pushing the stick forward to rock the glider off the single wheel, to the wooden skid underneath. Speed rapidly falls off and I try to keep the wings level for as long as possible. There is nothing worse than watching a glider come to a stop by pirouetting around one wing. It causes damage too! That was it. My first flight over in two minutes. I felt great. For two minutes I had been the captain of an aircraft, a Kirkby Cadet glider registered XA282.

I must have shown a little promise because I was invited back to the gliding school (No.635), to undergo further glider pilot training, and flew many more times, including eight more solo flights. I even qualified as a winch operator, launching others into the wide blue yonder. On occasion, I used to drive the land rover, towing out the cables from the winch to the other end of the runway. I wasn't too good at driving and spent most of the time either stalling or lurching down the runway.

Other highlights of my cadet career included playing the Last Post on Remembrance Day, in the Anglican Cathedral in Liverpool. I felt very proud to be asked to do that. I have, and always will, do my utmost to attend a cenotaph parade on Remembrance Sunday, to remember those who made the ultimate sacrifice for their country and for others, whatever their uniform and wherever the conflict. I also represented the North West England cadet region at diving and high jump competitions. I was unbeaten at high jump until the arrival of a boy called Alex Kruger. He took over the mantle of ace high jumper, eventually going on to be included in the British national team competing in the Olympic Games. I still disliked him at the time though. Also, I rose to the dizzy heights of cadet sergeant. Cadets aside, I had a full and varied childhood and, fortunately for my parents, spent most of my adolescence sleeping.

School was plodding along quite well. Nothing too good to shout about, but enough to get me behind the controls of a helicopter. I was in the school athletics team (Doing well, until the arrival of Alex Kruger), so spent probably more time thinking about sport rather than education. I did, however, manage to bluff my way through my mock 'O' level exams. School was OK, I enjoyed the majority of it. It was a mixed comprehensive school about two miles from my house. The walk to and from was always interesting, as there were plenty of opportunities to endear ourselves to the local community.

However, one day, the date I cannot remember although the day will remain with me forever, my life was to completely change. I was in class, filling in some gap of knowledge between mock exam and real exam, when we were told that we were to be the subject of a school medical examination, prior to leaving school. Nothing unusual in that I thought.

A good excuse to get out of lessons. We stood in a line outside of the office being used by the nurse. As usual, the regular group I hung around with began to fill in time by amusing ourselves and annoying the teachers.   Word filtered out that someone ahead of us in the line was colour blind. I had never heard of it. What did it mean? Never mind, we thought, and continued to be stupid. We decided that a colour-blind person would be unable to tell the difference between a black and white person, and that at least they could save money by buying a black and white television. There was no way I was colour blind because I was a glider pilot, and I knew that pilots required perfect vision. Surely I was OK.

My turn eventually came and I presented myself in the sparsely furnished small office containing the nurse. She did not look up as I entered and spoke only to ask my name. After finding the appropriate piece of paper with my name on, she carried out the usual height, weight rubbish and then pointed to a small, square shaped book lying open on the table. On one of the pages was a white square of card, on which I could see a circle made up of a number of dots. Most of the dots were grey in colour but a few of them were orange. The orange ones made the shape of the number twelve. With an almost casual wave of her pen, in the direction of the book of dots, (she had yet to look at me), the nurse said, "What number do you see?" "Twelve." I replied. If this was the colour-blind test, it was easy. "Well carry on then." said the nurse. I turned the page and saw two different circles of dots. I stood there and said nothing because there was nothing to say. I saw nothing to talk about. "What are those numbers?" asked the nurse. "What numbers?" was my obvious reply. Again, without looking at me, she turned the page and asked me to try again. At this point I could feel a panic begin to rise in me. I was fighting to remain calm when matter-of-factly, the nurse said, "OK, You're colour blind. Send the next one in." She had wrecked my life and she still hadn't looked at me. "No, wait a minute, I can't be colour blind because I fly gliders and I want to join the RAF as a pilot." was all I could think of saying. I was informed in what was a very cold manner that I would had to choose a different career and could I please send the next one in as there were a lot of people to see, and it as getting near to lunchtime. I left the room in what could best be described as a daze. What was I going to do? I had never considered any other occupation for my future.

I don't remember much between leaving the nurse's office and lunchtime. As soon as the lunchtime bell rang, I picked up my bag and left to walk the two miles home, even though I normally stayed for school lunch. So many thoughts were going through my head. How was I going to tell everyone? What was I going to do? I must have gone into mixed emotion overload! The following weekend I was due to attend the Officer and Aircrew Selection Centre at RAF Biggin Hill. I even had the travel warrant, issued the week previously from the RAF Careers Information Office. I remember walking down the road towards home, desperately trying not to burst into tears. I had been bullied at school, and had resolved never to let them see me cry or get upset. I was damned if they were going to get a free show! I made it to the house and broke down in floods of tears. The house was empty because everyone else was either at school or work. I eventually telephoned my mum at work and told her. She allowed me to have the rest of the day at home and said she would get home when she could. This was a major vote of support, as to be allowed time off school usually required a visit from the Grim Reaper. Nothing less would do. I spent the time on my own looking toward the future, but there was nothing to see. I had convinced myself, and everyone else, that I was going to join the RAF. I had no contingency plans.

My parents and brother eventually returned home and offered encouragement and support. At the time, it made a great difference, but looking back, I think it actually did much more. It kept me sane. I was booked an appointment with an independent optician who checked my eyesight thoroughly, but confirmed the diagnosis. He was far more sympathetic though. Although I had seldom seen it, I knew my dad was very capable in the 'letting off steam' department. He took time off work and arrived at school with me one day. Word went around the school that there was a Mr. Angry, looking to speak to the Headmaster. Of course, he was busy, so the Deputy Head offered herself up for sacrifice (presumably on the assumption that Mr. Angry would not thump a female). Dad would never have hit anyone anyway. When faced with a hand wringing Deputy Head he exploded, but remained in complete control of the situation. Answers were required at to why this kind of examination took place so late in the academic career of children, so close to final examinations, thereby leaving occupation choices in jeopardy. He refused invitations to go somewhere for a quiet chat and demanded answers to his questions. I don't recall any forthcoming. The only good that came out of the visit was that policy was changed to ensure that the colour-blind test was carried out soon after the child joined the school. Too late for me but at least no one else would have to go through what I was going through.

With support from family, I telephoned RAF Biggin Hill, myself, to explain that I would not be attending and apologised for wasting their time. I was told that many people only found out about being colour-blind when they had an eyesight test as part of the selection medical examination. I was glad I found out when I did! I spent the next few weeks, keeping myself to myself, not wanting to talk to anyone, but knowing fully that my family was there if I needed them. Although I still attended school, I had given up because I felt I had nothing to aim for. Revision for exams did not go as planned but I didn't care. After a short while, if I am truthful, I felt obliged to still join the RAF because I had told so many people and I didn't want to look stupid. It was those thoughts that took me back to the entrance of the RAF Careers Information Office in London Road, Liverpool. I had been here many times before, but this would be the first time I had entered for anything other than being a pilot. I spoke nervously to a very pleasant airwoman, sat behind a desk, and she arranged for me to speak to her sergeant. I mumbled something about not worrying if it was too much trouble, but she remained cheerful and insisted I waited just a few minutes. Had I left at that point, I doubt I would ever have returned. True to the airwoman's word, a sergeant appeared from an office toward the rear of the building, asked for me by name and took me into the office from where he had previously been.

The walls had posters all over the place. I tried not to look at them because I knew most would be about flying. As I recounted why I was there, looking for a trade other than flying, it was all I could do to stop myself from crying. I explained my situation to the sergeant, who remained quite positive and reassuring. He told me that his name was Pete Geoffs. I found him a likeable man. He reassured me that the RAF did employ people who were colour-blind, and that he would find out what was available for me.

I returned at the appointed date and time and sat the standard RAF entrance examinations. After marking, I was told that I had scored very well. I asked what trades were open to me and said that if I could not fly an aeroplane, I would like to work as an engineer on one. Sergeant Geoffs told me that I had severely limited options available to me due the severity of my colour perception. Unfortunately, he said, there were only three trades open to me. Those were supplier, general duties and medical assistant. Sergeant Geoffs advised me that a supply airman was basically a warehouseman, a general duties airman was a gofer (go for this and go for that) and that a medic was a valuable asset to any station. He went on to expand on the role of the medic, and placed it higher in status than the other two options (I later realised that each trade is as important as every other). I thought if I'm going to join, it might as well be as the best of what is on offer. I wasn't convinced, but I still wanted to save face. I took the medical assistant information sheets away with me to read some more. Inwardly, I wasn't sure what I wanted to do anymore. Outwardly, I maintained the illusion of being RAF super-keen. A few weeks later, I returned to the Careers Information Office and, again, spoke to Pete Geoffs. He was as enthusiastic as ever and continued to promote the medical trade. It was then that he revealed that he was a medic. No wonder he was selling hard! I decided to take the plunge and sign up. After filling in more forms, swearing the allegiance, I was given a starting date of 23 September 1980.

I had finally joined the Royal Air Force. I was sure I would find out what the full role of my chosen trade would be after a few months. But had I made the right decision?

Chapter 2

I had now committed myself to joining up. Between finishing my time at school and starting the RAF, I worked as a sports equipment salesman in Jack Sharpe Sports Shop in Liverpool City centre. It wasn't much but I was grateful to them for taking me on short term.

All of a sudden, 23rd September was upon me and I found myself walking along Bowring Park Road toward the railway station to catch my train to Lincoln, and then on to RAF Swinderby and basic training. I was happy to walk, as I didn't want anyone to stand on a station platform and wave me off like in one of the old black and white films. After an uneventful trip, I stood nervously with others waiting to be collected by military coach and taken to camp. I remember sitting on the coach, gazing out of the window as it turned to pass through the large metal entrance gates, and thinking, "What have I let myself in for?" I was soon to find out. It was a little like a scene from an American film. We stood in a line after getting off the bus, to be met with our new "Mother", (He really did say, "I'm your Mother now."), a tall thin corporal by the name of Corporal Bowden. I never did find out his first name! He stood there in his immaculately pressed uniform, creases in the trousers that could have been used for shaving, and the shine on his boots would have served as the mirror. There was one peculiarity though; he wore an eye patch. My instructor was a pirate! He barked his orders at us without pausing for breath, allocating us rooms, bed-spaces and giving us instructions of where to be and when to be there. All this included a static guided tour of RAF Swinderby, and it was accepted that we had understood all. "Any questions, no, good, fall out." Was his parting shot, again without any pause for breath. It actually sounded like, "Anyquestionsnogoodfallout!!" We were to have the pleasure of his company for the next six weeks. Deep joy.

RAF Swinderby was the Royal Air Force's basic training camp for all non-commissioned airmen. Even airmen aircrew had to undergo the basics here. Airwomen were trained at RAF Hereford in Wales. Corporal Bowden was the flight Corporal for number Five Flight, my flight. It was his job to instil both military and self-discipline and basic military knowledge into the most raw of recruits. The senior NCO in charge of the flight was Sergeant Nicholls. The only difference between him and Corporal Bowden was that he could shout a little louder, and devised slightly more evil punishments for us should we, in their humble opinion, so deserve! Five Flight was no different to either Four or Six Flights (our total intake for the month). There was a mixture of ex-military, ex-Air Training Corps cadets, people with no former association whatsoever and the odd airman who, for whatever reason, had been back-coursed to our intake. We settled into our eight-bedded room and started to unpack what little belongings we had brought. It would only be a few days before we would be issued vast amounts of uniform to pad out our nearly empty lockers.

Corporal Bowden was a ferocious man. Any weakness or insecurity was punished severely. There was never any physical bullying, but the verbal assaults were horrendous. You could always tell when the new intake was in because they had not been issued with their uniform. The more senior intakes saw it as a boost to themselves, because a new intake meant that they were that much closer to passing out of Swinderby. A process I very much looked forward to myself. I had been given a little inside information because my brother, Alec, had not long been in the RAF himself. He had joined as a RAF Policeman and was at his first station, RAF Neatishead, in Norfolk. I followed his advice and did as I was told by the instructors, trying hard not to get noticed. After about three or four days, we were marched across to clothing stores to get our initial kit issue. Working our way down the longest counter in the world, we collected vast amounts of items of clothing. The issued kit ranged from socks through to full camouflage clothing. I am sure it was issued in such an order so as to make it almost impossible to stack and carry without dropping anything. Of course, the large kitbag was issued last and placed in the top of the unstable pile! We were doubled back to the accommodation block, leaving a trail of clothing items behind us. After an immediate kit inspection, several of the flight were seen scurrying back towards clothing stores to retrieve lost items. What followed then was like something that you would see in a comedy film. Although only 17, I knew how to dress myself and other such basic functions of life. There were recruits who could not tie their tie, didn't know how to lace up their boots, and would walk around with their beret like Table Mountain. Corporal Bowden and Sergeant Nicholls were almost hoarse by the end of that day!

Strangely enough, as if by magic, there appeared in the accommodation block a station photographer, who kindly offered to take photographs of us in our new uniforms. For a small fee, of course! It never occurred to me that in such a tight training schedule, there was always time for the photographer to visit. Still, I joined the queue and posed for mummy. I'm sure she was proud. Photographs over, Corporal Bowden announced his arrival with the usual screaming and shouting. We were Five Flight and our motto was 'We like pain.' I'm sure he took that as an order. He certainly enjoyed inflicting it. His reasoning was that if you felt pain it showed that you were alive. We settled down to the training routine of drill, polishing, cleaning and the instillation of discipline – both military and personal. Five Flight had to be better than the other two flights on our intake. We had to be that much better at drill, presentation and attitude. Any failings were punished severely both by Corporal Bowden and others within the flight. On our floor of Gibson Block, (a new building), the bathroom floor was tiled. Each intake, under the guidance of Corporal Bowden, took turns to redo the grouting between the floor tiles. It was our turn to paint them from white to black. We had a "Bull" night every evening, where if you stood still long enough, someone would come along and polish you! The fire extinguisher, dustbin and linoleum floor were all in everyday use but resembled mirrors. Even our issue kit did not escape the Bowden treatment. Our mess tins doubled as mirrors, the soles of our shoes had to be as shiny as the tops, our belts were trimmed so that only 1" remained through the gleaming brass belt buckle, and the paint on the brass eyelets of our boots was scraped off in order to give us some more brass to polish. We would never need to shoot the enemy; we could just stand in the sun and blind them with our reflection. Kit inspection took place every Thursday. Every single item of issued kit was laid out on your bed and inspected. It also had to conform to the poster showing the appropriate layout. Failure to stick to the layout, dirt on any item of kit (no matter how small the speck of dirt), untidiness or even just for the hell of it could see your kit being thrown unceremoniously across the room. I remember one Thursday my entire kit and mattress ended up being thrown out of the window because there was a speck of dirt on the bottom of one shoe. Not bad to say we were on the first floor! Quite often you would be standing to attention by your bed, either being inspected or nervously waiting for your turn, when you would see someone's worldly possessions whoosh past the window, having been assisted outside by the helpful inspecting staff from the floor above. At least we were all suffering. Still, as the weeks progressed, we gradually improved as individuals and gelled together as a group.

During the course of our training we were given instruction on the use of weapons and nuclear, biological and chemical (NBC) warfare protection. This training was delivered by the much feared RAF Regiment, or Rock Apes as they were affectionately known. The Rocks were the RAF's soldiers, whose primary task was that of defending an airfield or deployed Squadron, during times of conflict. They thrived on their reputations of being tough and mean. Especially to new recruits! Our NBC clothing consisted of charcoal-backed trousers and hooded smock, rubber gloves and overboots and a respirator (God help anyone who called it a gas mask!) In order to demonstrate the effectiveness of our NBC clothing we were taken to the 'confidence chamber', otherwise referred to as the gas chamber. We would go inside in small groups, fully clothed in our NBC kit. Once inside the Rock instructor would light one or two (usually three or four) small tablets of CS, a chemical irritant used in crowd control. It causes severe pain to the eyes and throat, but the effects wear off fairly quickly. There were about a dozen of us in the chamber and the CS tablets had been lit. It hissed as the white smoke drifted upwards into the wafting arms of our instructor.

Once he was happy that there was enough CS in the air, we were taken through the drills for decontaminating ourselves and each other. This required massive amounts of Fullers Earth, an inert powder that would soak up any contamination. We were also given instruction on eating and drinking drills. This is where people began to panic. They were petrified of breathing any of the CS irritant in, so stopped thinking. The drinking drill required you to take a deep breath in, lift your respirator off your face and take a gulp of water from a water bottle that had been decontaminated with Fullers Earth. You then replaced your respirator, swallowed the water, blew out as hard as you could and decontaminated around your face again. We had people breathing out before swallowing the water and then panicking as the water level rose to half way up the eyeglass. The next thing they did was rip off the respirator to breath in. They then remembered the CS irritant and started coughing and spluttering even more. The same procedure is used for eating, but this time we had flakes of cracker biscuit filling the respirator! Our instructor would fling the door of the chamber open and unceremoniously throw the recruit out. However, they soon came back in again to get it right. Right at the end of all the drills, we took it in turn to take our respirators off, recite our name rank and number, and chosen trade before being thrown out of the chamber, tears and snot streaming down our face and gasping for fresh air. This was to prove that our equipment really did offer us some protection. I'm sure it was also to amuse the Rock Apes!

We were, of course, all going our separate ways following basic training. I remember there being other potential medics on other intakes, but none in Five Flight. Each flight had a senior recruit, responsible to the training staff for the flight as a whole. Each room had an allocated room leader who was responsible for the cleanliness, tidiness and anything else that took place within that room. For some unknown reason, even at seventeen years of age, I was made our room leader following the unceremonious "sacking" of the initial selection. Quite a challenge as some of the older recruits and those who joined us from previous intakes were not too enamoured with my appointment. In reality, it was just another reason that the training staff could make your life uncomfortable. "Room leader! Why is that man's bed a mess?" More often than not followed by my kit taking another flying lesson, even though it was someone else's bed that was a mess. All good character building stuff they said. Our morale was continually improving as we progressed through the six weeks. Newer intakes were arriving every week, reinforcing the fact that we were ever closer to 'Passing Out'. Soon it was our turn to be the graduating recruits. We had finally made it through. On the way, we had lost some to injury, medical conditions discovered after enlistment and simply some who found that the military wasn't for them. The military lifestyle doesn't suit everybody, so I would never criticise those who tried and left. I do, however, have no time for those who criticise without even trying.

The weather was cold but dry for our big day. We formed up, ready to march on to the sacred parade square, in front of the seated crowd of proud families and friends. Corporal Bowden was displaying his vocal prowess, psyching us up so that we were at our best. The band struck up and we were off. I felt so proud to be marching to a military band, a feeling which never left me, regardless of how many years I had been in. The parade passed without a hitch. Orders were barked out and complied with immediately. The stamping of the feet sounded as one and not like our first attempt which had resembled a machine gun. Awards for achievement were presented, and the obligatory fly-past took place. We were lucky to have the magnificently graceful Vulcan bomber for our day.

After being dismissed for the final time at RAF Swinderby, there was plenty of patting each other on the back, shaking of hands and a great sensation of achievement. There were times that I disliked being at RAF Swinderby, but they were overshadowed by the good times. After the mutual congratulations were exhausted, we found our families and set off for the refreshment building. I introduced my parents to the now infamous Corporal Bowden, complete with eye patch, and prepared to leave RAF Swinderby for my new posting to the Institute of Community and Tropical Medicine, at RAF Halton in Wendover, Buckinghamshire. That was to be a place that I would revisit on many occasions in the future.

Royal Air Force Halton was a massive station. It was home to the technical training establishment, apprentice training, all medical training and the home to Princess Mary's Royal Air Force Hospital. My home for the next sixteen weeks was to be the old plastics and burns unit, which was in the hospital grounds. We now had the luxury of only four to a room, but it was like sleeping and living on a hospital ward. It was also full of brass fittings! Discipline was still in evidence as we were still recruits. Not only was there brass everywhere, there was miles of linoleum. It all had to sparkle. My trade instructor was a corporal called Stu Russell. You could tell that we were getting further into the RAF because we found out the corporal's first name! Also, airmen and airwomen began to train alongside each other. Stu Russell was a tall, slim

Irishman, who's favourite saying when you got something wrong was, "Your Arsehole!" He was an excellent trainer. During the most boring of lessons, he would liven them up with the odd story of what he used to get up to prior to becoming an instructor. He had a Citroen 2CV motor car, which baffled him completely. He knew he had to put petrol in it but that was all. Many a time he would tell us that something else had gone wrong on his car, and did anyone know what the problem could be? That aside, he knew his medical subjects inside out, and imparted it with great skill. We were taught the basic subjects such as first aid, basic medical administration and basic nursing skills (similar to that of an Auxiliary Nurse).

My time at RAF Halton was during the time that the Irish Republican Army was blowing things up in the London area. We were all told to be extra vigilant for things such as unattended packages or parcels. Being recruits, we were exceptionally vigilant. I woke one morning and staggered off to the bathroom, as usual, only to find everyone in the communal area walking around half asleep, yawning and bleary-eyed. One of the others in the block told me that they had spent most of the night standing outside of the accommodation block. When I asked why, he looked surprised and asked if I had spent the night elsewhere (even though we had to stay on camp overnight). When I said no, he looked a bit puzzled. He told me that a suspicious package had been found alongside our accommodation block and that the explosives experts had been called out to assess the package. It had been decided to carry out a controlled explosion by shooting it with a remote shotgun. That would see if it went bang or not. The parcel had been found under my window! The recruit who had been tasked to clear the block had made his way through the block shaking awake anyone found in bed. I had been missed because I was such a skinny sod and had sunk deep into my deep hospital mattress that my bed looked like it was empty. Also, I was in such a deep sleep, that I didn't hear anyone shouting or moving about. I had, therefore, been left behind. I thought I was the target of a wind-up, as was the common practice in the block, until I went back to my bed-space and opened the curtains. There up the window was a rather large soot-type mark. The first in a list of narrow escapes.

As mentioned, wind-ups were a common occurrence in our block. We were a good mix of people who, on the whole, got on very well together. It was common practice to gently lift someone's bed onto four chairs, or bedside lockers whilst they were still asleep. Then we would raise their wardrobe by the same height. After that, one of us would stand on a chair and shake them awake, telling them that they were late. Usually, a cursory glance at their alarm clock (which we had changed) was followed by them leaping out of bed and plummeting to the ground some three feet further down than was anticipated. Perhaps you had to be there, but it was incredibly funny. One lad woke to find his entire bed-space in the corridor. On the following intake, there was a bloke whose personal hygiene was a little lacking. His alarm clock would go off first thing in the morning and, before he even opened his eyes, he had a lit cigarette in his mouth. We never saw him in the bathroom or have a wash. Ever. We complained to the training staff, but there was little change. He never appeared to wash his clothes either. They always ended up in a heap at the bottom of his locker. One weekend this bloke went away when the majority of us stayed behind. We clubbed together and bought about six large cans of anti perspirant and some sellotape. The cans were sellotaped together and the spray nozzles sellotaped in the 'spray' position. One of us had to prise the top of Mr Smelly's locker open whilst the rest of the team made the aerosol bombs. Not long after, his locker was gently hissing and a fine mist was filtering through the crack between the two doors. I don't know what was worse, the original smell from his locker, or the combination of six different brands of anti perspirant. We were, however, immensely proud of our first successful military operation. He never said a thing when he came back. Initially, there was a puzzled look on his face as he tried to work out where all the empty cans came from, but he was expressionless when he placed the 'bombs' one by one into the waste bin. Perhaps he didn't know what they were! It made him freshen up a bit though (or was it just the after-smell of our bombs?

The training continued and more first aid and administrative skills were developed. As part of our basic nursing care phase, we had to spend a month on the wards in the hospital. I have to say I hated it. We were nothing more than little run-arounds for the student nurses, who because they were in the RAF, (or PMRAF in their case), had either the rank of LAC or SAC. In their mind we were mere AC's, and because we were going to be medics, they saw us as some form of inferior life form. We were given all the menial jobs such as washing bedpans and damp dusting the bedside lockers. Occasionally, if we were lucky, we may be able to take a temperature. Most of the time we were given pieces of paper to fill in or medical records to fetch and carry. I had taken to the trade of medic and felt that I was gaining experience and confidence on almost a daily basis. I disliked the way we were being treated and the stupidity of some of the student nurses.

I was witness to a poor man, after having both big toenails removed, being woken up by a nurse slapping the bottom of the bed where his feet were. It worked as an alarm call though! She claimed to have forgotten what his operation was. I suppose he was lucky that it wasn't a vasectomy. I was walking past the bed of another man who had had an operation on his leg. He didn't look too well so I took a peek under the blankets. The drain had fallen out and he was sitting in a fair sized pool of blood. Having fought my initial panic, I approached a trained nurse in the office. The patient was duly treated and I was told off for overstepping the boundaries of my ability. Obviously I was not qualified to lift blankets. The divide between the medics and the nurses was getting bigger by the day and I was delighted when I made a particularly bad nurse cry after she made up an answer to a question I had asked. What had upset her was the fact that I had taken great delight in pointing out her stupidity and lack of knowledge. My pride lasted until matron had a word with me for upsetting one of 'her girls'. After that, I just took a dislike to nurses.

My sense of fun was developing at an alarming rate. We used to have wheelchair races around the wards, diving under the over-bed tables and weaving around man made obstacles such as patients in chairs. If a patient was rude and they were on traction, their weights would be swung until an apology made. Metal bedpans were placed in the freezer prior to being placed under the stroppy patient. Usually, after the initial shock had registered, they seemed unable to use the bedpan.

Fortunately, the month on the ward was soon over and we were back in the classroom environment and the usual words of encouragement – "Your Arsehole!" There was now only one course of trainee medics ahead of us and they would soon complete their training and be posted to their first station. On the whole, they were good-natured and we all got on well together. As usual, there were instances of personality clashes. Mine was with a brummie called Mark Alder. We had clashed on a few occasions, most notably in the local pub, the Rose and Crown. He had taken a bite of my burger and annoyed me immensely. As he went for his second attempt at eating my burger, he found one of the pub darts sticking in the back of his hand. From that point on we were destined not to enjoy each other's company! The same night, I was rudely awoken by what felt like a shove on the side of the head. As I came around, I saw Mark Alder walking off down the corridor with a glass bottle in his hand. As in any argument, I had to have the last word. I jumped out of bed and set off after him, calling politely that I would like a word. This caused some of the others to wake up, and I was soon at the bottom of a pile of bodies trying to prevent me from getting at Mark. After the dust settled we all went back to our beds. After all, Mark was on the course ahead, and would soon be posted away, hopefully never to be seen again. Mark's course completed their training and it was, for them, time to leave. I was glad, not only because Mark Alder was going, but that made us senior course and one step closer to completing the training.

I was ironing my uniform one Friday evening when Mark Alder approached me. His uniform had been returned prior to posting and his tunic had his new propeller sleeve badge of the rank of Leading Aircraftsman or LAC. Big as ever, he stood by the ironing board, thrust his tunic at me and said in his broad brummie accent, "Just call me LAC." Unfortunately for him I was a bit too quick and grabbed his head. Holding my nice hot steam iron close to his face, I advised him, in the finest military terms, that it would be best if he were to go away. He did. After he left that weekend, we never saw each other again for eleven years. Neither of us complained.

In one month it would be my turn to leave. I hoped that I would be posted to a flying station, as the latest trend was for medics to get posted to hospitals and non front-line stations. I would find out soon enough. All I had to do was successfully complete written and practical exams in first aid, basic nursing techniques, medical administration, dispensing and anatomy and physiology. The exams went quite well and there were not too many "Your Arseholes!"

I had managed to complete the course, finishing second overall. Not bad for someone who, twelve months earlier had never heard of the trade, or shown an interest in a caring profession. After finding out that we had all passed, all we wanted to know was where we would be able to perform our new found skills. We sat in the classroom, more nervous than at any other time, waiting for the commanding officer to come in. Corporal Russell brought us to attention as the CO swept into the room. We had the usual speech telling us how well we had done and all other such hot air. They knew we were only interested in our postings. Good news, they were flying stations and, being quite keen, I knew what flew on most of the stations. I still hoped for helicopters though.

"Dixon. You're posted to RAF Church Fenton." Where the hell was Church Fenton? I had never heard of it. More importantly, was it a flying station?

"Where is it and what do they do there, Sir?" Was all I could manage as a reply.

I was told that it was in North Yorkshire and that it had recently re-opened as a basic flying training station for all student RAF pilots. Who said God didn't have a sense of humour. They flew mark 3 and mark 5 Jet Provost aircraft. Great, I will have to face the very people I had dreamed of emulating, and be in the part of the RAF which dealt with the Morris Minor of jet aircraft. Still, the name being called after mine was being posted to the RAF Hospital at Wroughton near Swindon.

There were one or two tears from people who didn't like their posting, and from some whom were a little unsure about leaving the safe environment of the training school. However, on the whole everyone accepted their lot and set about completing the end of course administration. A few days later I was standing on the platform of Wendover railway station, travel warrant in hand, waiting for the train to Church Fenton in North Yorkshire. It wouldn't be the last time I stood on the platform at Wendover, or visited RAF Halton.

<u>Chapter 3</u>

I remember it being a bright sunny day as the train rattled along the track towards Church Fenton, a small village in North Yorkshire. The land was reasonably flat and the visibility quite good. Some ten minutes out from the station, I stood by the door of the train, waiting for it to finally arrive at my new home. As I looked out across the green fields, separated only with hedgerows and dry stone walls, I saw a red and white Jet Provost flying low and level, and parallel with the train. I have to admit to feeling a little flutter of excitement in the pit of my stomach at the first sight of a part of my new station. The train duly arrived and, after collecting my kitbag and other property, I set off up the steps to the station exit. I was aware that I would be met by a medic from RAF Church Fenton who would take me to my new home and my new career. I left the station and saw a tall, slim spectacled airman, with the telltale medical insignia, known as a caduceus, on his collar. As I approached, I offered my hand and said, "Hello Corporal, I'm LAC Dixon. I'm very pleased to meet you." He looked a little puzzled as he shook my hand. Then a large smile crossed his face as he replied, "I'm Sam. What's your proper name?" My first encounter with a human NCO! Sam Perry was a very pleasant man. He was single and lived in one of the blocks on the camp. He was to become my early mentor and good friend. Eventually, I would have the honour of being best man at his wedding.

After bundling all my kit into the rear of a sherpa van, we set off on the short drive through the village, toward the camp. After no more than ten minutes we turned in through the large blue metal gates which had the words RAF Church Fenton along the length in big gold letters. I was finally in the proper RAF. We drove straight to the Medical Centre where I was introduced to the staff. The Station Medical Officer was Flight Lieutenant Jeremy Watson-Cooke, an extremely pleasant man with a wicked sense of humour and little regard for all the politics of a commissioned rank. First and foremost, he was a doctor. Senior NCO in charge was Sergeant "Chick" Korran a short, stout Scot who, on first appearance, gave the impression he was about to tear your head off. It was, of course, the completely wrong impression. He only did that if you got something wrong! Corporal Sam Perry was the Junior NCO of the Medical Centre. The remaining staff consisted of Senior Aircraftsman (SAC) Clive "Boris" Benson, Senior Aircraftswoman (SACW) Gail Edmonds and a SAC nurse by the name of Garry Gibbons. Garry was as mad as a March hare, but exceptionally good at his job. He restored a great deal of my faith in the nursing profession after my unimpressed introduction at Halton. It was rumoured that Garry had once been a

Royal Air Force Regiment gunner prior to re-mustering to his present trade. After all the pleasantries had been exchanged and a mug of NAFFI tea had been thrust in my hand, I was given a tour of my new workplace. The Medical Centre at RAF Church Fenton was a single storey building, which looked as if it had been built in the 1950's. It was quite spacious although all the space was utilised to the full. There was a doctor's consulting room, treatment room, patient's waiting room, dispensary, storeroom, staff rest room and duty room. Also, all the usual amenities such as kitchen, bathroom and the like. My accommodation had been arranged, prior to my arrival. It was to be in a multi occupancy room with five other blokes, all different trades. I was also told that I would be the Medical Centre receptionist when I reported for duty the following morning. This was the usual practice for the new starter. Boris was to be my mentor for the first few weeks. He would give me the 'pep-talk' on day two. I was then taken back to my block and allowed the rest of the morning to unpack all of my kit. After lunch, I went to the Medical Centre and was immediately made to feel part of the team. I would settle in soon, I thought.

Boris met me for breakfast the next morning and set about his task of mentor. I don't think that he had looked after a LAC before because all he could talk about was me being his junior and how he would be training me to do as he said. All the time he kept punching his fist into his other palm, as if to reinforce what would happen to me should I decide not to do as he said. Unfortunately for him, he didn't scare me at all. I nervously sat at reception on my first morning, and began booking appointments for those wishing to report sick for that day. Later in the morning, I was called into Sergeant Korran's office. I though that maybe I had got something wrong, but it was to tell me that I would be going on a course at RAF Hospital Wroughton in a month's time. I had been nominated to do my electrocadiographers course. No sooner had I arrived at my new unit, but I was to be away after only a month. Oh well, never mind. Sergeant Korran explained that it was quite unusual for someone so young in service to get such a course. I can't remember if I was pleased or not. Over the next month at Church Fenton, things went well. I began to learn my trade; both by experience and tuition from those I worked with (even Boris). Garry Gibbons taught me basic nursing techniques. He was a red haired man from Hull who wore a large unkempt moustache, which made him look more like an invading Viking, rather than an exceptionally talented nurse. He was also very loud, and possessed possibly the worst sense of humour I had ever encountered. Regardless of whatever injury or illness he was faced with, Garry was composure itself. I don't recall ever seeing him get into a flap about anything. He also possessed a wonderful skill of sobering up immediately if, when drunk, someone needed his services, although he never drank when on duty. Unfortunately for me, that was one trick of Garry's I could never master – sobering up, that is. I never drank alcohol on duty either.

Anyway, at the point where I was just finding my feet, I was again packing my bags and setting off for RAF Wroughton. This was a strange feeling because all other courses I had undertaken were as a recruit on basic training. On arrival for the course, I reported to the General Office who assumed I was a medical LAC being posted into the unit. Once informed that I was on a course the clerk became more polite and issued all the necessary admin. RAF Hospital Wroughton was a large, two-storey building set in a large expansive area of Wiltshire. About a mile away, but still on the site, was an airfield used by the Fleet Air Arm. The other side of the airfield was the married quarters. Unfortunately for us, there was no accommodation available to us in the airmen's blocks as they were undergoing redecoration. Instead, we were going to be housed in one of the married quarters. This was fine because we were so far away from the hospital complex; we could let out hair down without causing too much trouble for ourselves. The only downside was the mile walk to breakfast and work each morning. It wasn't long before we started exploring the area and were delighted to find that the road out of the back of the married quarters led to the local village which, unfortunately, contained nine pubs. Regrettably, the first three of these pubs were closer than the bar in the NAFFI club on camp. The course itself was quite interesting. It took me a few days to accept that I was on a normal training course and not one run by individuals who talked at you with the volume on maximum. You were also allowed to speak yourself! The senior instructor was Sergeant Jim Bolton, a very pleasant man who, I think, looked after me due to the fact that I was not long out of the wrapper. The evenings were spent mainly in the village, sampling the wares of the local hostelries. Our favourite was the pub called The Iron Horse, although we referred to it as The Rusty Donkey due to the décor. I was making the most of my newly acquired taste for alcohol. The weekends were particularly horrendous. Only one bloke on the course had a car, an Austin Princess bought for him by his mother. We did little during Saturday and Sunday, due to being too fragile after the usual attempt of trying to get from one end of the village to the other, stopping in each pub and sampling a different pint in each. It was, of course, a trip out and a trip back. I don't recall ever having a successful mission. I do recall giving up trying to walk up the one-in-six hill at the rear of the married quarters, and sleeping under someone's hedge for the night! Still, the month long course was uneventful and enjoyable.

On the last morning of the course, five of us jumped into the Austin Princess and headed off to the reception area of the Hospital, to begin our station clearing procedure. It consisted of being given a small blue card with a list of different departments that we had to visit. Once there, checks were made to see if we owed anyone money, gave back all loaned equipment, and generally give others something to do. As the car pulled up outside of the hospital we all got out. However, before we had chance to reach back into the car to collect out kit, the car drove off. We were left standing, cursing the driver, as we now had to walk to the car park to retrieve our possessions. So much for an early start. We had taken barely one step, when a window at the front of the hospital flew open. We heard the voice long before the head and shoulders of the Hospital Warrant Officer catapulted her voluminous torso through the metal window frame. "Airman! Where's your beret?" she bellowed.

"It's in the car Ma'am." Was all I could think to say. "Well it should be on your head!" I don't know why, but my reply to her next question sent her into a complete rage.

"What? The car? It'll break my neck."

Her voice raised about two octaves and two hundred decibels.

"Be in my office at five o'clock!"

We scurried off struggling not to burst into a fit of giggles, as we knew we were leaving the hospital at three o'clock. Course administration finished, we were given the final examination scores, and found that we had all passed. After the farewells, we made our way quietly passed the Hospital Warrant Officer's office and off the unit to freedom.

I had the weekend off, but telephoned RAF Church Fenton to make enquiries about returning for the Bank Holiday Monday which followed. I was so new to the RAF I was unsure whether the Bank Holidays were worked or not. I spoke to Sam Perry, who was a little amused at my naivety. He also asked me if I knew a medic called Donald Dougal. I said I did and refused to comment on what he was like as he had been there a fortnight and nobody could work him out. In fact, I think I refused to return to the unit on the Tuesday. I had known Donald through basic training, as he had been on the course behind mine. He was a likeable person, but gave the impression of being completely useless. I don't know where he had spent his life, but he was completely out of his depth in reality. After my weekend at home, I returned to Church Fenton to see Donald for the first time since

Halton. I thought he must have improved, as otherwise he wouldn't have passed al his final exams. Although only a month and a half had passed since I had seen him; he was identical to my last memory; even down to how his hair stood up as if he had just got out of bed. I'm sure he modelled himself on Sonic the Hedgehog. I was pleased to see him though, as it meant that I wasn't the new boy any more. Unfortunately for me, people thought I was the new boy as I had only been there a week before going off to Wroughton and Donald had been there for a fortnight. I settled quickly into the new way of life and soon found my way into the medical stores area of the medical centre. It was probably because I went into stores so early in my career, that I enjoyed it so much. Initially, I made a complete mess of it. We ran out of medicines, things were going out of date before there was a chance to use them and other such stupid mistakes. However, after some expert tuition from Sergeant Korran's replacement, Sergeant Mike Jarvis, I became proficient in the duties expected from me and stores became a good place to work.

I was also now undertaking duty medic duties, which included being on duty for a 24-hour period, and being first on call for any medical emergencies. On our duty weekend we were on duty from Friday morning until Monday morning. It was a tour of duty we all hated. My first ever incident was a chef who had cut his finger, quite badly, whilst opening a tin can. Thankfully I was able to deal with that by myself. A few weeks later, I was on duty during the week, when a young airman came hammering on the door. As I answered it he blurted out, "My wife is having a baby in the house." I immediately called the duty doctor, only to be told by his wife that he had just stepped into the bath and could I go and deal with the situation until he was able to meet me at the address. Trying hard not to join the soon to be father in a state of panic, I collected whatever equipment I thought I would need, and ran to the address. I ran in through the door and was directed up the stairs. There was no one in the bedroom! Husband then ran up and said, "She's not in here, she's on the toilet." I had visions of me having to pull junior from the U-bend. I persuaded mother to leave the bathroom and lay on the bed in the position I had seen in the first aid books. I could see the baby's head was starting to appear. Pity it wasn't the doctor's head. After what seemed five lifetimes, the doctor arrived and safely delivered the two month premature baby. Mother and baby were transferred by ambulance to the local hospital, where sadly, a few days later the baby died. I was absolutely devastated and shed the odd tear or two, although being careful not to show how upset I was to my colleagues.

Still, there were always the antics of Donald to cheer us up. He was easy to play tricks on. If he was on the telephone, and you took hold of the cable and tied it in a knot, he thought the signal could not get through and would hang up. Another time, I gave him a broom and told him that the glide path on the airfield needed sweeping. Most people knew that the glide path was the bit of airspace between the flying circuit and the beginning of the runway. However, I got in a bit of trouble after Donald was picked up by an Air Traffic Control Assistant, having been seen walking down the middle of the runway happily sweeping his brush. The ATC Assistant was a

SAC called Simon Naylor, and we were to become very good friends over the years.

Part of our duties also included providing crash rescue assistance in the event of a Jet Provost, or any other aircraft, crashing on or in the vicinity of the airfield. I enjoyed this part of the duty immensely, as I had an opportunity to climb all over the aircraft.

There were 'practice crashes' called on a regular basis. I don't think Donald ever got to grips with the map reading and airfield navigation as he used to disappear for ages when on a practice which, more often than not, was usually within the airfield boundary. How he could miss three massive RAF fire engines, lights blazing and a red and white Jet Provost aircraft in the middle of a big green field, I will never know. We also used to have various states of declared emergencies. Emergency State Three was usually a minor problem, which required the emergency crews, (fire and ambulance) to be manned up only. Emergency State Two required the vehicles to be manned, but report to a given location somewhere on the airfield, usually somewhere near the intersection of both runways. Emergency State One was either a smoking hole in the ground, or the likelihood of a smoking hole in the ground. Normally, States two and three resulted in a stand-down as the aircraft landed safely. We all became a little complacent about them. I was sat at the intersection of the runways on one such State Two, and had taken my mug of tea with me. I sat with the driver watching the familiar shape of a Mk5 Jet Provost approach the end of the runway. Our message had been that there was a problem with the undercarriage. As it came closer, I counted the three undercarriage legs with all wheels attached. Another boring few minutes, I thought, and sipped at my tea. We had also been told that the pilot was a student and that this was his second solo flight. As the aircraft touched down, all appeared well until a few seconds later when it slewed to the left, and off the runway. "Emergency State One, Emergency State One." Came the message across the radio. No kidding, I thought. We set off after the aeroplane and the fire engines. The Jet Provost was skidding across the grass, bumping up and down. At one point I thought it might turn upside down. However, the pilot inside must have been doing the right things, as it righted itself and continued the skid. It slammed into the ground as the pilot retracted the undercarriage. As the aircraft began to slow, I jumped out of the ambulance and ran towards it. As it came to a halt, I was aware of one of the firemen standing next to the canopy, which was beginning to open. I believe the fireman had jumped onto the wing as it had slid past him, and he hung on for the ride! Anyway, the canopy was open and I was now on the other wing. The fireman was switching off all the battery, fuel pump and engine switches while I reached inside and took one of the ejector seat pins out of it's stowed position. The pins were designed to fit into various places on the Martin Baker ejection seat and stop it from being fired by accident. The main one was called the Main Sear and was situated behind the top of the seat, to the rear of the pilot's head. It was sometimes a little fiddly to get to. The second pin was the Seat Pan Handle pin. This was the loop, which stuck up between the pilot's legs. As with all emergency equipment, it was yellow and black striped so as to make it easy to see. The pilot who had just brought the aircraft to a halt was now quite keen to leave the cockpit. I pushed him back into his seat, even though the harness was still securing him to the seat and attempted to put the seat pan handle pin into the safe position. As I was placing the pin in, the pilot reached down with a pin of his own and kindly stuck it into the back of my hand. I was too hyped up with adrenaline to notice at first and continued to pin the seat prior to getting the pilot out. Once all the important pins were in, the pilot was brought out by two firemen, whilst the rest of their crew gave cover in case a fire broke out. With the pilot safely out of the aeroplane, my job was to get him to the medical centre, so that he could be checked out by the Doc. I remember thinking how strange a Jet Provost looked, sitting on the floor without any undercarriage. Fortunately, the pilot suffered no long-term injuries as a result of the incident. Sadly, he was to be chopped from the course a short while later, as he failed to meet up to the required standards.

This incident reinforced the need for medics to be able to react to incidents on the airfield, both during the day, and the night. Donald Dougal did not get on too well with navigating around the airfield, or using the radio. It was decided that he would be sent on a practice emergency during a night flying exercise. So that he could not use the excuse of following the fire engines, he was told that the pilot had ejected over the airfield. He was, therefore, given a different map reference to the fire crews. Simon Naylor would play the part of the ejected pilot and the ambulance driver was Senior Aircraftwoman Pauline Rowley. I was courting Pauline at the time, and we would eventually marry. I was to co-ordinate the 'rescue', so was stood in the air traffic control tower at about ten o'clock on the night in question. The airfield controller pressed the emergency button on his control pad, and the result was the emergency telephones in both the fire section and the medical centre ringing simultaneously. The practice crash message was passed informing all of the whereabouts of the crashed aeroplane and the ejected pilot. The darkness of the airfield was suddenly broken by the headlights, four way indicators and flashing blue lights of the fire engines leaving their station on the edge of the airfield. We looked towards the direction that the ambulance should arrive from and waited. Shortly, we saw the ambulance approach the airfield, and drive straight on, without obtaining permission from the controller. The ambulance too, was lit up like a Christmas Tree. Pauline had been told about the planned exercise, and had been briefed not to correct any mistakes Donald made, as he had to learn. The ambulance soon fell in behind the fire engines, until the controller reminded him that the pilot had ejected, and was at a different location to the one the fire crews were going to. The ambulance stopped for about five minutes whilst Donald worked out where he had to go. Things weren't going as smoothly as I had planned. Eventually, the ambulance set off in what appeared the right direction, only to stop on the grass alongside one of the runways. Without taking a torch, Donald then got out of the ambulance and set off running across the grass to find the casualty. Simon Naylor (the casualty) informed me later that the only reason Donald had found him was because as he was running through the knee-deep grass, Donald fell over after accidentally kicking Simon in the ribs. Having found his casualty, Donald now had to find the ambulance again. Even with all the flashing lights, he could not see it. The casualty gently pointed him in the right direction, as he wanted to go home, because his ribs hurt. As Donald arrived back at the ambulance, Pauline was less than happy. She asked where the casualty was but Donald couldn't remember! Driving in the direction of where Donald had just run from, they spotted Simon Naylor jumping up and down in the beam of the headlights. He was convinced that he would have been run over if he hadn't. Simon lay down again while Donald got the stretcher out of the back of the ambulance, and between him and Pauline, attempted to lift the casualty onto the stretcher. Pauline lifted the feet up, but Donald appeared to be having problems with the top end. Only when Simon let out a yell, did Donald realise that he was standing on the hand of his casualty, and therefore, could not lift him up properly. After what was about an hour and a half, the casualty was in the back of the ambulance, and heading for the medical centre. The air traffic controller was not best pleased, as a five-minute practice had closed his airfield for about an hour and a half. Simon also refused to play casualty again, as he had the beginnings of hypothermia, bruised ribs and a sore hand!

I had my share of getting in trouble too. On one station exercise, I managed to get myself in trouble on no more than three different incidents! The first was when I was positioned by the door of the medical centre, acting as the guard and triage officer. A man, wearing civilian clothes approached. I knew he was Distaff (Directing Staff), as he carried a clipboard and wore a white armband on his left arm. He knocked on the door and as soon as I opened it, indicated a direction with his pen and said, "There's a fire over there. What are you going to do about it?" He had indicated toward the area where all contaminated waste, both medical and human, would have been buried in a pit, were this a real incident.

"Nothing," was my reply. "That's the shit pit, and shit doesn't burn."

"Well, further over there." was the umpire's flustered reply.

"Hang on there then." I muttered before sauntering off down the corridor. I returned, dragging a red water/gas fire extinguisher behind me. As I left the medical centre and headed off to the fictitious seat of the raging inferno, the umpire hurried alongside of me and said, "OK, I just wanted to see if you knew which fire extinguisher to use." I held out my arm and said, "Stand back please, this could be dangerous."

At the same time, I broke the seal on the top of the extinguisher and hit the plunger. The extinguisher spluttered into life. I casually hosed down the burning wall, turning to the umpire to offer a smug grin. He seemed less than pleased with my performance thus far. "Alright then, you have put the fire out. How do you stop the extinguisher from continuing to spray water?"

"That's easy, just turn it upside down." I replied. As I did so I let go of the short length of hose in order to get hold of the bottom of the cylinder. Unfortunately, the hose swept across the umpire and soaked him from midriff to head before hissing to a stop. I was trying desperately not to laugh as the now furious umpire began scribbling on his clipboard. The worst bit was when his pen ripped through the soaking paper. He stormed off and left me to return to the building, carrying my now empty trophy over my shoulder.

The second of my day's triumphs occurred after the medical centre had been put under pressure by the arrival of a number of 'battle casualties'. My primary task, whilst at the door, was to assess and triage all casualties. In other words, put them into an order of who was to receive treatment first, depending on their injuries and staff available to treat them. There were four priorities of casualty, with each being allocated an identifying colour. Priority one (Red), was in need of urgent life saving treatment. Priority two (Blue), was next, with a need for urgent treatment, but could survive a little longer. Priority three (Green), were classed as the walking wounded, and poor old Priority Four (Black), being advised not to start reading any long books (or already dead). The standard practice in identifying who was what priority was to mark the forehead of the casualty with the appropriate coloured marker indicating T1 – T4. That way, a quick glance at the forehead of the casualty indicated where in the medical centre they would be taken for treatment.

Unfortunately for this group of casualties, I had become bored. I had swapped the casualty marking pens with indelible ink ones. They were all assessed and marked for treatment, as usual, but only I knew what lay ahead for them. Pity I didn't know what lay ahead for me though! One of the 'casualties' was the Station Navigation Officer - a Flight Lieutenant. He had been assessed as untreatable and therefore 'T4'. His forehead, which had been extending backwards for a number of years, had been duly marked with a large black T4. During the course of this casualty influx, the Station Commander paid us a visit to see how we were coping. He was shown around out set-up by the Doc, and appeared quite happy with what he saw. During the course of his walkabout, the Station Nav approached him and pointed out that he had been killed off. He asked the C.O. for permission to leave the exercise and go home to work on something or other. The Station Commander gave his permission, but advised that he might like to wash off the large T4 adorning his head prior to leaving. After washing his head in a small sink in the treatment area, he made the fatal mistake of asking me if the T4 had been washed off. Of course I said yes, even though it was still there in all it's glory (albeit a little damp). The Station Nav left us, happy as a sand-boy, with a little skip in his step, no doubt thinking he had got one over the establishment as he had been allowed to leave before the end of the exercise. I had thought that his intention was to go home and work. However, prior to him going home, he decided to do a bit of shopping at the local supermarket. He had put a civilian jacket over the top of his uniform and gone straight from the exercise. I don't think he made it home before he came blazing back onto camp. His whole head was as red as a beetroot, (with a black T4 written on it), he was that mad. He demanded to know what I thought I was doing. I replied that I was unaware of what had happened to the marker pens and that I had been too busy to really notice when he asked me if the T4 had been washed off. By a miracle, I got away with it. Apparently, he only noticed when he was at the fruit display which was the kind with the angled mirrors at the back of the display. As he reached forward to collect some fruit, he was met with a backward written T4 on top of a head, which looked remarkably like his. It then became clear as to why most of the other shoppers had been sniggering as he walked around doing his shopping. After he had left for the second time, a decision was made to take me off the door and give me something to do inside the treatment area. At least someone could keep an eye on me!

Unfortunately, several hours later, I was put back on the door. We were now a long way into a very boring exercise. After an even longer period of inactivity, and watching student pilots walking around the camp, carrying pickaxe handles, pretending that they were rifles, I was more bored than I had ever been. A Tannoy announcing "Air Raid Warning Red, Air Raid Warning Red" broke the boredom. Suddenly a couple of RAF jets screamed overhead. Shortly after that I was told that we could expect up to 20 casualties, and most would be arriving on a converted stretcher-carrying coach. As the coach pulled up, a long line of people came around the corner and headed for the door of the medical centre. A Squadron Leader banged on the door. As I opened the door, he attempted to barge past me but my foot was behind the door and he came to a juddering halt.
"We have to come in because there's an air raid!" he screamed, sounding as if he genuinely believed that we really *were* under attack.

"You'll have to go somewhere else because a coach load of casualties has arrived, and they take priority." was my reply.

"I demand that you let us in!" he countered.

"No. Go away. We're busy." was my nonchalant reply. By now, the Doc was aware of what was going on at the door, and being keen for me not to cause any further trouble, told me to let them in. The Squadron Leader looked at me and pushed at the door. It still didn't move. "Go over to the bunker and clear your weapons before coming in." I said to him. He then started arguing about the time it would take and for me not to be ridiculous. I said to him, "It's the Geneva Convention."

He replied, now angrily, "I think that's pathetic." By this time I had had enough of him and snapped, "Why don't you piss off and phone Geneva then!"

Just before he exploded, Sam Perry replaced me on the door and I was sent into the depths of the medical centre to await the arrival of the casualties. Apparently he kept looking for me whilst he was in the medical centre so that he could deal with me. However, the Doc had made us all wear chemical warfare suits and respirators so that we all looked the same. Another close escape!

The were numerous times when I sailed close to the wind, but was lucky enough not to get in serious trouble. Most of the time it was just sheer stupidity. One day in winter, Garry and myself tied some wooden planks to our feet and tried to ski down the steep sides of the decontamination centre. We both got about two feet down the slope before the planks dug into the ground and catapulted us into the snow after a short arc shaped flight. Amazingly, we walked away without a scratch.

I had also got a lot closer to Pauline, the regular ambulance driver, and on October 23 1982 we were married in her home village of Ollerton in Nottinghamshire. It was a very special day which, coincidentally, was also my Dad's birthday.

A couple of other memorable incidents involved being called out to a train that had derailed and rolled down an embankment. Fortunately, the most serious incident was a broken wrist. It could have been a lot worse! The second memorable incident was on the airfield and involved the three Pitts Specials aircraft of the Royal Jordanian Air Force Display Team. They were coming into land a few minutes after each other. The first was directed to land on the right hand side of the runway and turn left. The second aircraft was directed to land on the left hand side of the runway and turn right. The poor sod in the third aircraft had nowhere left to go. He landed and had to apply the brakes in such a way that the small aircraft tipped up and slid along the runway on its nose and undercarriage. An emergency state one was declared and we all turned out. The pilot was still strapped into aircraft number three and had aviation fuel leaking over him. I 'shimmied' up the fuselage to transfer some weight to the back. At the tail hit the floor, I fell off. Before I could get up, the pilot had unstrapped himself and was storming off across the airfield to, we presumed, give a piece of his mind to the air traffic controller. Several of the firemen grabbed hold of him and the Doc managed to persuade him to come in the ambulance to the medical centre for a check up. He was, fortunately, OK and had calmed down enough not to go off and cause damage to a controller.

RAF Church Fenton was, looking back, a fantastic place to learn my new trade and settle down into a life away from home. I had met my wife and experienced numerous medical situations, from aeroplane crashes to train crashes, and emergency childbirth to sprains and strains. One of the strangest incidents happened on a weekend when, whilst outside the medical centre washing Pauline's car, a male screeched to a halt in his own car and shouted, "Come quickly. Someone has been hit by an aeroplane." I must have had a puzzled look on my face, as I knew that there was no flying that weekend. However, he appeared in such a panic, I jumped in the car with him. We sped off back to the airfield where, I suppose I imagined I would see a smoking hole in the ground with the odd arm and leg sticking out. We pulled up and people were frantically waving me towards where they were. I still couldn't see (or hear) any aeroplanes. As the crowd parted I saw a young lad, lying on his front, with a large remote controlled aeroplane literally sticking out of his lower back. The whole front of the model (including propeller) was inside him. I felt the old familiar feeling of surging panic beginning to rise, a split second before the medical training kicked in. We got him back to the medical centre and I immediately called the civilian ambulance out. We had a civilian GP on call that weekend and I knew there would be little they could do, and would probably arrive at the same time as the ambulance anyway. Whilst I was waiting for them to arrive, I used the shears normally used for cutting off plaster-casts, to cut away the part of the aeroplane not inside the boy. I then flooded the hole with sterile salt-water solution to dilute any fuel that may have leaked inside the cavity. The hole was big enough to put my fist in. Using a torch, I could see that, miraculously, there appeared little internal organ damage and I was surprised at the lack of bleeding. I covered the hole with sterile dressings and safety pinned a blanket around the boy in such a way that the blanket supported the weight of the model engine. Fortunately, the ambulance arrived shortly afterwards and took the lad off the York District Hospital. I understand that he made a full recovery.

After being at Church Fenton for two and a half years, I had fooled everyone into thinking that I knew what I was doing. I was lucky enough to be selected for promotion to Corporal. I would have to attend a General Service promotion course at RAF Hereford and return to dear old RAF Halton for a Trade promotion course. Only after successfully completing both, would I be able to be promoted. I also knew that I couldn't stay at Church Fenton. The question was where would I be posted to? I didn't want to go too far because we had bought a bungalow nearby and I wanted to stay there. Pauline had also left the RAF and was training to be a nurse at the local hospital. Then came the posting notice. On successful completion of both courses, I would be posted to RAF Staxton Wold. Another station I had never heard of! Were they trying to tell me something? As I had never heard of it, there was always a chance it wasn't a flying station either. Things were looking grim.

<u>Chapter 4</u>

RAF Staxton Wold turned out to be a small radar station stuck on the top of a large hill in the middle of the North Yorkshire Moors. It was a small, but important, link in the United Kingdom strategic air defence chain. Unfortunately, it was a non-flying station. It appeared to be a very old station, with drab coloured square buildings positioned throughout the small wire-fenced complex. There was a large sweeping radar called, I think, a Type 85. This was situated on top of a building and had a large elliptical shaped dish, which revolved at a given speed. I was told that it had become too heavy for the supporting building and that cracks were appearing throughout the structure. Also on the site were a couple of height finding radar towers.   These consisted of lengthwise elliptical radar dishes moving in an up and down configuration. Our task was to identify and track any Eastern European missile launches and aircraft movements and, play a part in co-ordinating the countermeasures and aircraft intercepts of the West. I really did not know too much about the inside of the main complex, as it was a secure and classified area, and although I had the security clearance to enter (in the event of a medical emergency), I rarely used to go in. I thought the less I knew, the better. Plus the fact, it was such a hassle getting into the building. I was sure one of the first missiles would have Staxton Wold written on it, so that further missile launches would go undetected. Most of the time, Staxton Wold was surrounded by cloud or bad weather. There would have been little point looking out of the window to see what was happening. Although we were only about 15 miles from Scarborough, and at the top of a big hill, the weather only cleared once that I recall, when I could see the seaside resort.

As I have already said, RAF Staxton Wold was a small station. So much so, there was no room for a permanent medical centre. I was stationed some 15 miles away at an Army camp called Driffield. This was home to the Junior Leader training camp for the Royal Corps of Transport (RCT). The only other RAF person on Driffield was a painter and finisher called Gordon Dobson. He was also a Corporal, and was as pleased to be on an Army camp as I was. We hit it off straight away. I had never served with the Army before and it took a little getting used to at first. My first observation was that it was a far more disciplined environment than I had just come from. That said, Five Flight at Swinderby had given me a good grounding in self-discipline, so the further transition wasn't too traumatic. It was also quite strange going to a new medical centre on promotion, and having no one to practice my new supervisory skills on. Still, at least I could make my mistakes without anyone else knowing.

The medical centre was little more than three rooms in an otherwise unused building. One room was my office, another was the Doctor's office and the third was the treatment room. On average, there was about three patients a day. Not too stimulating. However, most of my time was spent undoing all the mistakes left by my predecessor. There were medical documents missing, routine medical examinations and specialist appointments overdue, and loads of medical equipment missing.

I tried to get to Staxton Wold at least once a week, so that I knew my way around, and other personnel would at least know who their medic was. This would come in handy for when we were to go on exercise (or to war), as I was to be part of a first aid reaction team. What made me laugh was that the senior man in the first aid team had to be a Sergeant. Our team leader was a radar technician! Handy, I suppose if someone got electrocuted. It must have been quite intimidating for him at times, but to his credit, he always allowed me to take the lead. I was also medic to a small search and rescue flight based at another Army station called Leconfield. Sadly, I only managed to visit them once. Another satellite unit was the aircraft live firing range called RAF Cowden Range. This was a small airfield on the Humberside coast, where various aircraft would fly to and simulate a ground attack with bombs and guns. I managed two visits there and was fascinated each time.

I remember one day standing in the control tower at Cowden Range, looking out over the target area, when the radio buzzed into life. There was a distinct American accent to the pilot. After his conversation with the controller, it was explained to me that an American A10 Tankbuster would be simulating a ground attack over the range. I was told which direction the A10 would be coming in from and I kept a lookout until I was able to see it begin the approach. The graceful aircraft - the result of an airframe being designed around a gattling gun, swooped towards the targets on the ground. There was a puff of smoke from the front of the nose area, followed about half a second later by what sounded like the rasping of a chain saw. The ground around the targets then erupted with numerous miniature explosions, and the targets were ripped to shreds. That sight was followed by the noise of the rounds impacting on the ground, which in itself was devastating. I remember thinking at the time that I would hate to be on the receiving end of that. Little did I realise that in six years time I would be at war, at a forward operating base, sharing an airfield with a squadron of these awesome machines. Back at Cowden Range, the next aircraft in was a Dutch F16 Fighting Falcon. As far as fast jets go, this is my favourite so I was looking forward to seeing one of these in action. Again I watched the approach, which to me, appeared a little different from the A10's. The controlled asked me to move a little further to the right, inside of the small control tower. Without thinking, or taking my eyes off the aircraft I did so. The F16 continued to get closer. Suddenly the controller announced, "Stop, Stop, Stop. You are targeting the control tower. Do not continue. Abort, Abort, Abort." The F16 banked suddenly off to the right to go around and try again. My heart was in my mouth. Thinking that the controller had been concerned about my welfare, I asked him why he had asked me to move to the right during the last approach. He replied casually, "You were between me and the exit stairs."

"Oh, right." Was my only reply.

Back at Driffield, my friendship with Gordon Dobson had reached the 'play pranks on each other' phase. We felt a bond, being the only RAF guys. The pranks ranged from flower bombing each other from the roof of our respective work place, hoax mail, grease or other such substance on door handles to ink on telephone earpieces. My greatest triumph was when Gordon had left his spray bay to go home for lunch. I managed to get into the locked building by getting the keys from the guardroom, without signing for them. Had I signed for them, Gordon would have known that I had been in and sabotaged something. Because Gordon was usually covered in paint, he used an old pair of shoes for work and another clean pair of shoes for walking around the station. As Gordon had gone home, he had left his work shoes in his office. Knowing that I was operating within a short space of time (about half an hour), I quickly got into Gordon's office and set about sewing the front of his shoes to the carpet, using surgical suture silk. The shoes were left in the exact position that Gordon had left them in prior to lunch. The keys were then duly returned to the guardroom for Gordon to collect on his return.

I made sure that I was in the guardroom when Gordon returned. I engaged him in conversation and told him it was his turn to put the kettle on. We arrived back at the spray bay and I said that I would put the kettle on whilst

Gordon got changed. He pulled on his grey, paint covered, overalls, which he usually wore and kicked off his clean shoes. Without looking, he stepped into his work shoes and tried to walk off. The shoes stayed put but tipped forward at the toes. Halfway to the floor, Gordon resembled something like an Olympic ski jumper although, when he hit the floor he resembled Eddie the Eagle. I was almost crying with laughter as Gordon just lay there wondering what the hell had just happened. He had become separated from his shoes during the fall and they had fallen back into the place where he had left them. He thought he had tripped up over his laces until he tried to pick the shoes up off the floor. At that point he realised what I had done and set about attacking me. I made good my escape before he spray painted me olive green.

Work itself was fairly quiet. I had the occasional visitor with an interesting complaint, but in general it was routine coughs and colds. A soldier from the Parachute Regiment came in one day after cutting his hand on something. I saw it needed suturing and asked if such a tough bloke wanted local anaesthetic. He advised me that if he felt any pain, I would require a *general* anaesthetic! He never felt a thing.

Paperwork was a nightmare as the medic before me had not had much interest. There were medical documents all over the place. I had no doctor at Driffield, so had to use the civilian working at the other Army base at Leconfield. This doctor was horrible. A civilian working on a military base is somewhat indestructible. A civilian working on a military training establishment could get away with murder and this guy reveled in his elevated position. He thought of himself as somebody extremely important. Patients were seen in rank order, regardless of what their illness or injury was. He demanded to be called 'Sir' which sometimes was a little difficult for me. I had got into a habit of calling all my doctors 'Doc'. When he asked me why I wasn't calling him Sir I stated that I wasn't aware that he had been knighted by the Queen. I told him that anyone could become a Sir in the military, but the term Doc was a term of respect. Much to the disgust of the Army medics at Leconfield, I was the only one who ever got away with using the term Doc. I didn't actually respect him; it was my little rebellion. I wasn't over impressed with the Army medics either. They always seemed to either over-treat things, or ignore them completely. Instead of applying sticky strips over a cut, they would try and suture the wound. Either that or tell the patient it was nothing and to go away. Although I ended up doing duties there, I went to Leconfield as little as possible.

Driffield Army camp was used by the Army for driver training purposes. It was an old airfield, converted with man made hills, bumps and other terrain type features for the vehicles to drive over. One of the hills was a particularly severe 1:6. Following a long spell of rain, I received a call to say that someone had run themselves over on the driver training area. I had no idea how someone could accomplish such an achievement so turned out more from idle curiosity than in a medical capacity. On my arrival in the ambulance (driven by a civilian driver), I saw a soldier pressed into the side of the 1:6 hill.

It was as if he had just fallen back into snow. There was a perfect man shaped hole in the mud into which the hapless soldier fitted, with little other sign of damage nearby. The only other clue was a two-ton Eager-Beaver forklift truck, lying on its side at the bottom of the hill. The soldier was in a bad way. He was wearing a crash helmet, which had had one of the fishbowl type visors on. The helmet looked like a cracked eggshell and the visor had been ripped off, causing a bad laceration to the soldier's face. He was conscious and complained of pain all over his body. Apparently what had happened was he was trying to negotiate the 1:6 hill with his fork lift truck, carrying a heavy pallet. As he got half way up the hill, the truck started to slide in the mud. With the extra weight of the pallet at the front, the forklift turned sideways on and began to roll over. Normally, a sturdy cage surrounds the driver, so any unfortunate individual would have walked away from an incident such as this. However, on this particular occasion, the driver had left both cage doors open. As the forklift began to roll the driver elected to jump out. You or I would have probably jumped out of the top door so that the forklift would not squash you as it fell. Not so our embedded soldier. He thought the best thing to do would be to jump out of the lower door and run away. He forgot that the forklift would be right behind him. I suspected that he would have severe internal organ damage and the odd broken bone or two. I tried to gently lift the soldier out of his cozy recess, only to find he was stuck in a similar manner to that of our childhood wellington boot in a muddy field. Plenty of slurping sounds but no movement. Working quickly, I dug around his body shape in an attempt to get some air beneath his body, so that he could be extracted. This done, we threw him onto a stretcher with me cursing him for being so muddy in my nice clean ambulance, and set off at pace for the nearest hospital. Usually, I would have taken this kind of patient to the general hospital in Hull, however I decided that he was too badly injured and probably would not survive the trip. I told the ambulance driver to head towards the local village hospital in Driffield town. My thinking behind this was it would have doctors and medical equipment. The five minute journey took an age. His blood pressure was extremely low and giving me cause for concern. I had put a drip into his arm and kept him conscious for the journey. I didn't want to give him any pain relief, as I thought it would mask the symptoms for the examining doctor. Also, I couldn't give him any entonox gas as he had a head injury. At least his moaning let me know he was breathing. He was a gutsy bloke and coped very well with the journey. On arrival, I shouted at an ambulance crew near to the hospital entrance and asked them to give me a hand. The first came over, looked at my casualty and said they would get a medical team. The second came over and began shaking his head saying, "I wouldn't have brought him here. It's a village hospital." I didn't want to argue in front of the patient and to be quite frank; I had more important things to do at the time.

"Get hold of the stretcher and shut up." Was all I said to him. The medical team ran out to my ambulance and whisked the soldier away. I saw that they began working on him as they were rushing down the corridor. I gave my hand-over brief to a nurse before returning to my very muddy ambulance. The second ambulance man was waiting for me. He continued to criticize my decision to not go to Hull. I ignored him and set about tidying the back of the ambulance. He followed me inside and continued having his say. Big mistake! He was gently held by the throat, told (in military terms) to go away, and thrown backwards out of the ambulance. He picked himself up and ran around in circles shouting at me. At the suggestion of the driver, we made good our escape and cleaned the ambulance back at camp. I heard nothing more from the ambulance man, but received a letter of thanks from the hospital for the treatment given and making the right decision of where to take the casualty. The soldier had apparently required extensive life saving measures some two or three minutes after arrival at the hospital. He would not have survived the journey to Hull.

Back at Driffield, life continued in the same boring day to day drudgery of doctor's clinics and station exercises. One weekend in January it was the turn of RAF Fylingdales to have their station exercise. Fylingdales was another of the Early Warning radar sites used by the RAF. It was famous because of the much photographed big white 'Golf Balls' that stood out over the Moors. The exercise was to be held over a weekend because Fylingdales had a Royal Auxiliary Air Force (RAuxAF) Regiment squadron attached to them for defence purposes. The defence team from Staxton Wold had been selected to be the attacking force for the weekend. Gordon Dobson was in this team and suggested that I may like to go and play. I approached the officer in charge and suggested that it may be wise to take a medic with them. He agreed, and I was included in the team. On the weekend in question it snowed. It snowed as only it can on the North

Yorkshire Moors. We made camp at our forward operating base (a farmers field really, but this was the military!). After removing our equipment from the trailer, it became apparent that there were not enough tents to go around. Gordon and I set off for Fylingdales in a Land Rover. At the camp we told the guard that we were a Territorial Army unit on exercise in the area and that someone had been taken ill. Could we get a tent from the stores? We were given directions to the stores and spoke to the storeman on duty. Again, the same story was used and suprisingly he agreed to issue a tent. He asked what unit we were from so that he could book it out to our unit. He then issued a tent to a unit which, to this day, I don't think exists. Nonetheless, Gordon and I returned victorious to our base. The officer in charge then set about splitting us into pairs before giving us targets and missions to carry out against the defenders of Fylingdales. It was unanimously decided that following our previous success, Gordon and I should operate as a team. Gordon being Gordon then produced an old RAF flat cap that he had sprayed brown in colour, added gold beading to the peak, and painted a hammer and sickle on the front. He wanted to be known as Comrade Dobsonski. My request to be paired with someone else was refused amid howls of laughter. We were given two magazines of ammunition to go with our SLR rifles, and then given individual targets. Ours was the fuel pumps in the transport yard. We could attack when we wanted. After a mug of tea, we set off to assess the perimeter defences. We chose a point where two very bored looking sentries patrolled a stretch of approximately 100m of wire fence. The fence itself was only about three and a half feet high and straddled either side by uncut tall grass. Ideal. We timed their patrol for about an hour and then waited for the sun to set. At the given time we would run forward, hurdle the fence and hit the ground in the long grass. If that proved successful, we would then crawl to a predetermined point and begin the infiltration. If we were compromised at that point, we would simply jump back over the fence and run away. We lay motionless in rain and snow waiting for the sun to set. I was convinced the sun was staying up out of spite. Eventually, the time came when we could move and get some warmth back in our limbs. Watching the movement of the perimeter guards, we made our move. Sprinting towards the fence from about thirty yards away I saw Gordon, slightly ahead of me reach the fence and sail over the top before disappearing into the tall grass. I planted my foot to follow him over, only to have my foot disappear down a hole. I crashed into the fence and hung there like some damp washing over a washing line. I was a little shocked to say the least! Quickly gathering my thoughts, I rolled backwards and off the fence into the long grass on the outside of the fence. I lay there waiting for the guards to come and investigate what all the noise was but nothing happened. I could, however, hear Gordon rustling in the grass as he was trying not to laugh out loud. I crawled away and waited for the guards to go around their route again. I cleared the fence on my second attempt and met up with Gordon. There were white lines down the camouflage cream on his face, where tears had run following my first hurdling attempt. He greeted me with the international wanker sign. Crawling forward, we got our breath back and waited to see if we had been detected. All was OK. Crawling up to one of the camp buildings, the light had now faded completely and there were no lights showing inside the camp area. We hid in one of the ditches alongside the building and waited. As we were orientating ourselves, a lone radio operator walked around the corner. I don't think he had seen us, but he stopped and waited. It must have been one of those moments where you know someone is watching you but you don't know where from. All of a sudden, Gordon stood up. "Psst." he said, "Get over here, there's intruders on camp." The radio operator trotted over and jumped in the ditch with us.

"Tell control that they're down by the Sergeant's Mess." said Gordon. The radio operator passed the message and a short while later we saw their quick reaction force doubling away in the direction of the mess.

"Dickhead." I said to Gordon, "They were over that direction." And pointed in a completely different direction to that which the reaction team had run.

"What, the water tower?" asked the radio operator.

"Yeah, that's it." I replied thanking him silently.

The radio crackled into life and soon after, we saw the reaction force trotting off towards the water tower. Gordon then asked where the petrol tanks where and after casually telling us, the radio operator stopped suddenly and said, "You're the bleedin' intruders aren't you!"

All I saw was a white line of teeth as Gordon smiled. We tried to get the radio off the operator, but to his credit, he fought like a tiger. He started shouting so, discretion being the better part of valor, we decided to run away. We were not too far from the main entrance of the camp so took off that way. We ran down the approach road leaving the shouts behind us. Unbeknown to us, the water tower had been at the far end of the camp, so we had a head start on our pursuers. We ran past the sentry box by the front barrier. Inside the box was a Ministry of Defence policeman, who, by all accounts, refused to play at war. Later that night he was to become somewhat upset as another team crept up to his sentry box, tied rope onto the door handle, and waved at him as they ran round and round his box, tying him inside. They then showed him both ends of the cut telephone wire before running off into the night. Someone would be late off work that night!

Gordon and I cleared the main gate of the camp as the reaction force started up the road behind us. We could hear the blank ammunition going off behind us as they gave chase. We jumped into a ditch some 500 yards from the gate and tried to force some air into our lungs. A flare went up so we remained motionless apart from the heaving of our chests. A couple of loud bangs, interspersed with Anglo-Saxon cursing erupted as some more thunderflashes were thrown in the direction of our last known position. Thunderflashes are like bangers on firework night, only about fifty times as big. They can do quite a bit of damage if used carelessly. I heard a thud behind me and looked down to see a fizzing thunderflash on the floor about three feet from where I was.
"Shit! Run." was all I could manage before climbing over the top of Gordon, to get out of the ditch. We covered the top of the ditch as the bottom erupted in a shower of heather and mud. No one gave chase as we carried on down the road roaring with laughter.

The other teams had been having as much fun as we had, and soon a message was received by our officer that the defenders were getting a little demoralized by our activities and could we walk through an ambush to give them a victory. We all knew there would be a little bit of 'pay-back' from the defenders so drew lots to see who the lucky pair would be. Hurrah, it would be Gordon and me. We were given the co-ordinates of the ambush team and a time window of when we could walk through. We set off on the given route. There were no lights showing, so we made a little noise such as kicking the odd stone down the road. Graham was a smoker, so lit a cigarette and smoked it as we walked along. Nothing. We turned around and walked the route back the other way. This time we were a little louder, talking in a normal voice and laughing loudly. Still nothing. We checked the route to make sure we were on the right road. We were within the time window too. Our third pass had us kicking tin cans, dragging our feet along the road and Gordon was lighting cigarettes whilst stood in the road. When again, the ambush failed to materialize, we decided to go back to the tent and grab some sleep. It was later reported that the ambush team had set up in the wrong place! Never mind, we managed to get some sleep even if they didn't.

The next day was much the same. We managed to plant our 'bombs' on the fuel pumps and extract ourselves undetected. At one point we managed to steal the base commander's breakfast. Towards the end of the exercise, it was decided that we would have a combined final attack, with all pairs attacking different perimeter points at the same time. It would be a nice finale. We stayed in our original pairs and Gordon and I were given a section of wire to cross into camp. We were then expected to make as much noise as possible before being captured or 'killed' by the defending force. It was still quite dark in the early hours of Sunday morning, when Gordon and I made our way through the wooded area to the rear of the camp. Looking into the camp, we saw a small construction site, which had a four-foot high, crescent shaped mound of hardcore. It was decided that this would be where we made our 'last stand'. Quietly crossing the wire again, we took up positions at the mound. There was still a thin layer of snow on the ground that had now frozen, and each step we took crunched loudly. Still nobody came to check out the noise. Gordon picked up a stone and threw it against a building nearby. After a few more stones had followed the first, we heard the crunching footsteps of a squad of defenders coming our way. Making sure that we had a blank round of ammunition ready to fire, and the magazine was firmly attached, we positioned ourselves ready to shoot. As the squad came into view, we opened up. They ran in all directions and took up cover. Gordon and I didn't care. We kept firing in their general direction until we both heard the familiar 'Dead Man's Click'. This is the sound the rifle makes when you pull the trigger, and you have no ammunition left. In a live situation, it means you're dead. I looked across to Gordon, who was also out of ammunition. We both stood up and raised our hands. As the defenders cautiously approached us, we began to make our weapons safe: that is to apply the safety catch, remove the magazine and check that there are no rounds of ammunition left in the chamber. One of the defenders walked behind me and jabbed me in the back with the barrel of his rifle. He told me to put my rifle on the ground and out my hands up. I was under arrest. I told him that we were out of ammunition and were just making our weapons safe. We would not resist arrest. He jabbed me in the back again and repeated his one phrase. I told him the same answer, but added that if he prodded me in the back again, I would hit him. He did, so I felt obliged to carry out my promise. I hit him around the side of the head with the butt of my rifle and he went down immediately. I managed a quick sideways glance at Gordon before we were surrounded and 'forcibly' arrested. In other words, we got our heads kicked in! It was fun while it lasted. They took their frustrations for the previous two days out on us, but I suppose we had it coming. No complaints really.

Back at Driffield, I was, thankfully, more organized with my work and life continued along the usual routine, until one day, I was summoned to Staxton Wold. I wasn't aware that I had done anything wrong, but the way that Gordon and I had been carrying on, it wouldn't have surprised me. On arrival at the station, I went into the Admin Officer's office and was told that I was being attached to the Falkland Islands for a period of four months. There were numerous outposts in the Falklands, and I would be told where I was to work, on my arrival at the Islands. This would be my first detachment of any length. I wasn't looking forward to it. Pauline wasn't too pleased either. She had left the RAF a few years earlier and was soon to complete her nurse training at York District Hospital. My tour would run from September 1985 to January 1986, just over three years after the conflict, which had cost 258 British, 649 Argentine and 3 Falkland civilian lives during the 74 days of conflict. I would be leaving in just over one month's time.

The young hopeful, complete with helicopter landing pad beret! Alec will be as pleased at seeing this picture as he was when it was taken!

Sitting on top of one of the gliding school vehicles.
The winch is the vehicle to the right of the picture.
This was to be the start of my flying career

Taken whilst training at RAF Halton.
I had yet to earn my caduceus – the badge of the RAF Medic.

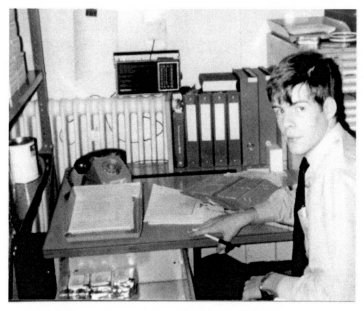

Training completed, I was posted to RAF Church Fenton
where I started work in the medical stores area.
Here I am trying to look busy.

Doc Watson-Cook was a great bloke.
This is the final battle in what had been a two-hour water fight.
As you can see, I was comprehensively beaten!

Taken on a families day airshow, a rare photograph of
Pauline driving the airfield crash ambulance. Corporal Sam
Perry can be seen walking away.

MOUNTAIN MEN
MT KENT
LIKE MOUNTIN' WOMEN

Guess where I was off to in 1985.
303 SU on Mount Kent, The Falkland Islands

A Hercules making an unusually high pass over Mount Kent.
The water tank can be seen behind the BV tracked vehicle and
the iso container.

Me walking off the helicopter landing pad at Mount Kent, after seeing off yet another 'Eric' Bristows helicopter.

Families Day in Hong Kong. Pauline leaves a Wessex of No 28 AC Sqn following a flight around the province.

Me on parade in Hong Kong. I'm at the end of the centre rank, just prior to the Staff Sergeant noticing that I was wearing my desert boots. He wasn't best pleased!

The Nepalese tailor who insisted on smartening himself
up prior to my taking his photograph.

I had never seen poverty on such a level. Here, a woman and
her child wash themselves on the street, using a water standpipe.

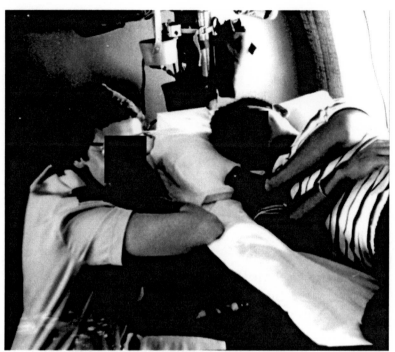

Sqn Ldr Evelyn Peters and patient, on board the RAF VC10 from Nepal to Hong Kong. Evelyn was the finest nurse I worked with.

St Martin's Church, Sek Kong, Hong Kong. Mark was christened here and Pauline and I were confirmed here by the Bishop of Hong Kong.

Chapter 5

My first trip to RAF Brize Norton would be the one that would take me furthest away from home. The Falkland Islands were some 9000 miles away in the Southern Hemisphere. We had found out, only a few days before I left home that Pauline was pregnant with our first child. I really didn't want to go.

After mulling around the departure lounge for ages, we were called to board the chartered Boeing 747 Jumbo Jet, still in it's British Airways livery. I boarded, and squeezed into the shoebox-sized space, which would contain me for the next sixteen hours. The only break in the flight would be a short stopover on the Ascention Islands. That was where the aircraft would stop to refuel, before continuing on to Port Stanley, capital of the Falkland Islands. Although it was good to get off at Ascention, I wanted to get the whole journey over and done with. It was a flight from hell, which lasted a lifetime. There was no in-flight entertainment, precious little food and absolutely nothing to do except sit there and wait for the flight to end. Port Stanley was a direct contrast to the Ascention Islands, being bleak, cold, windy and desolate. I remembered Ascention as having been warm and inviting. That said, I was glad that I was detached to the Falklands, as that was only a four month attachment as opposed to six for the Ascention Islands.

The arrival at Port Stanley was interesting to say the least. The hastily built runway was the same one used by the liberating forces. It was quite short as runways go. The wind was buffeting the aircraft as it began it's descent, until finally, with a heavy jolt, we had arrived. The roar of the engines increased as the reverse thrust further slowed the jumbo jet. As we taxied toward the arrivals lounge, I looked out of the window to see the reception committee of those waiting to go home. Our depression at arriving was countered by their excitement at leaving for home. As the cabin door was opened the cold air rushed in, reminding everybody of our new location. Leaving the aircraft I was pushed around by the invisible forces of the winds which swirled around the airfield. I was very impressed by the skill of the pilot who brought us safely down. In the wooden shed that was designated the arrivals hall, we were sat down and given an up to date briefing on the current political situation. Argentina was still posturing over the sovereignty of the Islands and there was still an air of tension between the two countries. We were also informed that there were still uncleared minefields on the Islands and, where they were known, minefield tape had been placed around the area. The officer in charge went to great lengths to tell us not to go inside these minefields. Sound advice I thought! He also advised us to let someone know if we found ourselves in a minefield that was, as yet, unchartered. The man was clearly a genius! After the initial brief was over, roll calls were made by different units claiming their new arrivals. Those of us going to outlying sties were to be accommodated on what was known as the 'Floating Hotel' overnight, prior to our transfer by helicopter the following day. I was off to a small radar site on top of Mount Kent. There were only seventy personnel on the site. I was the only medic, with the nearest doctor at Port Stanley some half hour by air or half day by surface transport. There were no formal roads to the mountain, so when flying was impossible, a tracked snowmobile known as a BV206 would be used.

We bounced about in the back of a small land rover and arrived in a mighty dust cloud alongside the 'Floating Hotel'. It was a container ship, with containers secured one on top of the other! I would spend my first night in the Falklands sleeping in a converted articulated lorry container unit. That said, it wasn't too bad. Three of us shared this small space. One was off to Ajax Bay, I was off to Mount Kent and I can't remember where the other was off to. I had heard of a few of the place names before, as I had been interested in the Conflict in 1982. Without telling Pauline, I had actually formally applied to be sent to the conflict area, in 1982, only to be told that that was not how the military worked. After an uneventful night on board the 'hotel' I returned to the airfield where I had arrived less than 24 hours earlier. The departure area was a wooden hut, which housed an incredibly bored looking RAF policeman. I was directed to a Sikorsky helicopter, which bore the name of the civilian company to which it belonged – Bristows. These helicopters, the lifeline of all outlying stations, became affectionately known as Erics;

their familiar red, white and blue livery standing out amongst the usual drab colour schemes of the military aircraft.

I remember feeling quite nervous when, after having strapped myself into my seat, the rotors of the Eric started to turn. I wondered what life would be like for me for the next few months and how would I be able to get home in a hurry should the need arise. Looking out of the small window as we took off, I began to see just how desolate, yet beautiful, the Falklands were. It was hard to imagine the fighting that had gone on three and a half years earlier. I felt that I owed those who died something, although I couldn't put my finger on what it was I actually 'owed'. As we flew west, the mountains stretched out before us. I soon realised that I was retracing, backwards, the route taken by the British Forces who had fought in the conflict and secured such a decisive victory. The capital of the Falklands, Stanley, appeared on the left. The red and green rooftops caught my eye as they stood out from the whitewashed walls of most of the properties. I caught sight of the Cathedral with its monument of whalebones forming an archway. Further on, Sapper Hill, also away to the left, came into view. This had been scene to one of the fiercest battles fought by 40 Commando composite battalion group, on the night of 13 – 14 June 1982. Keeping Tumbledown Mountain to the left, we flew past Mount William. On the same night as 40 Commando, the Scots Guards had courageously taken Tumbledown Mountain whilst 1/7 Duke of Edinburgh's Own Gurkha Rifles took Mount William. We then flew along Great Ridge, with Mount Harriet to the left and Two Sisters to the right before turning North West towards my home for the next four months, Mount Kent. Mount Harriet had been liberated by 42 Commando whilst 3 Para and 45 Commando regained Two Sisters. As a result of these, and other magnificent, hard-fought victories, the Argentine Commander General Menendez found himself surrounded by a ring of steel. British (and Nepalese) steel. Defeat for the Argentines was inevitable, with victory being secured on June 14 1982. The whole conflict had been a magnificent achievement for the British. It had only taken seven weeks to assemble and deploy 28,000 men and over 100 ships some 8000 miles from home. 10,000 men were put ashore onto hostile territory, who then took part in many battles against the enemy before bringing them to surrender in just three and a half weeks. I was three and a half years late but I felt very proud to be associated with such a professional and efficient organization. I said a silent prayer of respect to those who had given their life during the conflict.

Mount Kent loomed into view and the helicopter began its wind-buffeted descent onto the small square concrete landing pad. This was my stop. Once the crewman opened the door, I took off my life jacket (standard issue when flying over any water), and climbed down the steps. A bloke approached me, shook my hand and shouted over the noise of the rotor blades that he was the medic that I was replacing. He popped a hand-held radio into my hand, wished me luck and climbed aboard the Eric and took my seat! So much for a handover. A small gathering of airmen stood around the landing pad and applauded me as I walked to a safe distance from the helicopter. They then began a peculiar song and dance, although I couldn't hear what they were singing as the noise from the rotor blades increased as my 'taxi' took off for the next stop. Great, I was stuck 1500 feet up a wind swept mountain with a bunch of lunatics. The purpose of Mount Kent, or rather 303 SU was to operate the radar equipment placed on its summit, and to provide early warning of any unauthorized penetration of the exclusion zone around the Islands by Argentinean aircraft. There were two small golf ball like domes, which housed the radar equipment, sat on the highest point of the mountain. A short distance from the domes were a number of wooden buildings and more metal lorry containers, which was the living area of the site. I was taken to the medical centre building so that I could dump my kit prior to meeting the Commanding Officer, Squadron Leader Wilson. The footpaths between buildings were wooden pallets alongside which ran wooden handrails. On route to the OC's office I asked why that pallets had been used as a walkway.

"When it's windy, you have to crawl along on your hands and knees so as not to get blown off the mountain. You keep hold between the gaps in the wood." said my guide matter-of factly. Nigel Wilson was a very pleasant man who made me feel very welcome. After giving me the updated security brief, he went on to explain some of the other duties I was expected to carry out. I was responsible for issuing cold weather clothing, ensuring that there was sufficient clean bed linen for all seventy personnel, acting as helicopter marshal for all arriving helicopters (including being the fireman should anything untoward happen as the helicopter approached) and, most importantly, I was the postmaster for the site.

"Get the post wrong, and you'll be treating yourself." he said with more than a hint of truth in his voice. As I was the only medic on the mountain, with the nearest backup in Port Stanley, I was told that the personal radio I had been given during my 'handover' was so that I could be contacted at anytime. No sooner had I left the OC's office, the radio informed me that the next helicopter was due and could I go to the landing pad. Talk about hitting the ground running! Gazelle helicopter safely landed and dispatched, I returned to the medical centre to unpack my kit. It was a wooden building perched on the edge of the mountain, and it rattled and shook with the wind. The entrance led into the post room. On the wall was the sorting rack into which I would put the mail for individuals. On the table was a large pile of aerogram letters, affectionately known as blueys because of the blue colour of the paper. Blueys were the life blood of all who served overseas. On the wall was a poster, which listed the costs of sending parcels either by air or by sea. The window overlooked the drop down the north side of the mountain. The other door from the post office led into the medical centre, which, in fact, was a long portacabin. One end was the medical centre and the other was my living area. Apart from Squadron Leader Wilson, I was the only other person on the mountain who had a room to themselves. Luxury.

It didn't take too long settling into life on the mountain. My time was occupied with arriving and departing helicopters, and ensuring that everybody was keeping well. Each day I had to climb up a large water tower to take water samples. I would check these samples for chlorine levels. As there was no direct source of water for those of us on the mountain, it was pumped up and stored in the large tank. The result of the daily water test indicated how much chlorine powder I was to add, to ensure the safety of the water for consumption. Climbing on the tower was always a challenge in the howling wind and many a time I was nearly blown off the top, or through the hatch into the water.

Apart from the helicopters, there were Phantom jets and Hercules transport aircraft regularly flying around. To relieve their boredom they would often 'buzz' outlying sites, flying as close to the ground as possible. One morning I was on top of the water tower reaching in the tank to get the daily water sample, when I heard the usual rumble of a Hercules flying around. The noise sounded unusually loud but I put the change in noise down to the fact that I had my head inside a large water container and the sound was echoing around me. Having successfully collected my sample without falling off, or in, I stood up ready to kick the lid back on the water tank. The Hercules still sounded rather loud, and if anything, it was getting louder. I turned around to come face to face with a large transport aircraft heading straight towards me! I estimated that it would pass directly overhead at no more than ten feet. I considered jumping out of the way but decided against that option, as I would probably continue bouncing down the rocky mountainside. The Hercules continued towards me, growing larger and larger, until I could see both pilots grinning widely. I threw my legs from underneath me and landed flat on my back, still on top of the water tank, my water sample spilling all over me. The

Hercules thundered right over the top of my prostrate body. Eventually the noise subsided as the aircraft banked gently and arced gracefully around the two radar golf balls further up on the site. I sat up cursing the pilots and again collected the daily water sample. The medical centre was less than 200 meters away (the whole site was about 800 meters in length), and before I had got back, people were pointing and laughing at me. There was little else for me to do other than join in. Fortunately I had been observed doing the water tower flop, otherwise it would have been difficult explaining away the damp area on my trousers. I stood on top of the tower and took my bow as the Great Albert Dodger! The flying displays over the mountain were always very impressive and the majority of people would go outside and watch.

The Falkland Islands were still at a high state of alert and surrounding the radar site on Mount Kent were several sangars manned by guys from 47 Air Defence Battery. Should the need arise, they would protect the site from enemy aircraft with their shoulder mounted supersonic blowpipe missile. Fortunately, they were never needed in anger. One day we nearly had an embarrassing problem though. In order to keep the Blowpipe lads trained, a request used to go into the fast jet squadrons and ask for flybys from the Phantoms. It was the job of the Air Defence guys to simulate locking onto the aircraft and pretend to shoot them down. All went well and I enjoyed watching the way in which the Army lads operated. The missile was in a tube, over which fitted an aiming unit. The aiming unit consisted of a target screen, viewed through a binocular type set up, and a small thumb operated joystick on the right hand side of the unit. The operator had to fire the missile, collect it within the sight in two seconds and guide a supersonic missile onto its target using the thumb control. Impressive to say the least! During the fly-past the operator would go through all the drills of air defence, only stopping short of pressing the trigger. For someone who had never seen anything like this before, I found it fascinating. I was impressed by the skills of the Blowpipe operators and pilots alike, who were doing their best to evade the imaginary missiles. Later that day, one of the Blowpipe lads was walking around looking very pale. I asked him if there was a problem and he replied that there nearly had been. Apparently the safety catch on his aiming unit was not working and he had spent the best part of the afternoon, aiming at fast moving jets. His finger had been on the trigger most of the time, and a small twitch of the finger would have resulted in a live fire, that would have taken a lot of explaining. I was disappointed, as that would have been something worth seeing, but it did little to console him.

Mount Kent was also where I first came into contact with the Chinook helicopter. It was, and still is today, the workhorse of the British helicopter fleet. The Chinooks used to fly to Mount Kent on a weekly basis to take away containers full of the week's rubbish and deliver a new empty container for the week. It also brought us our fresh rations for the week. After having conducted the container changeover, it would land, lower the tail ramp and allow a human chain to form at the rear ramp to pass out the weekly rations. On one occasion, when most of the rations had been unloaded, I was inside the cabin area of the Chinook collecting the last few boxes. The loadmaster thought it would be a good idea to load me up with so much that I would have difficulty seeing where I was going. Unbeknown to me, or the loadmaster I was with, the second loadmaster had opened up the centre hatch to get ready to attach the full rubbish container. He had called for the aircraft to go into a hover of about 3 feet so that he could lower the hook in the centre of the aircraft. I walked forward with boxes piled high and rapidly exited the helicopter through the centre hatch. This was the second time that I had ended up on my back with an aircraft a couple of feet above me. Surrounded by all the boxes, my only consolation was that this time, it would not look like that I had wet myself. I was lucky to escape injury though. I can remember seeing both loadmasters looking down at me through the hole, almost crying with laughter. I responded with a hand signal that suggested that they were two feet above me! Leaving that experience aside, I thought back to my childhood, when I believed that I would be a pilot. Had I been able to, I would have loved to have been a Chinook pilot. I found the aircraft fascinating. Back in the UK, they were stationed at RAF Odiham. I would like to be posted there someday, I thought. Little did I know what was in store for me.

Life on the mountain was basic to say the least. We had basic washing facilities but little else. I remember one day a Chinook landed to drop off the weekly rations and once on board, I noticed a large washing machine all crated up. I pointed to it and told the loadmaster that it was for us.

He shook his head and said that he thought it was for Byron Heights, another radar site on West Falklands. I told him that he was wrong and that it was supposed to be for us. I took another armful of rations off the helicopter, and out of sight of the loadmaster, quickly wrote on my daily flight schedule that this Chinook was delivering a washing machine. When I got back on board I again stated my claim and produced the flight schedule. The loadmaster shrugged his shoulders and gave me a hand unloading our new washing machine onto the landing pad. I would love to know what he said to the lads at Byron Heights! Nevertheless, I was unit hero for about five minutes, until someone asked how we would carry this big heavy lump of metal along a windswept, narrow wooden walkway for about 700 meters. It was a struggle, I can tell you, but our now dented and scratched brand new washing machine was put to work immediately.

The high wind buffeting the mountain on a regular basis was a constant problem. During winter months, people would be blown over on the icy floor (resulting in catwalk diving awards being given in the Puffin Bar that same evening). The Puffin Bar was the focal point of the site. Rumor has it that when first built, everyone was inside watching a television that someone had shipped in. The wind blew the roof off during a crucial televised football match, and the subsequent snowstorm threatened to spoil the viewing. Apparently, no one moved at the disappearance of the roof, they just pulled up the hoods on their coats and carried on drinking. Such class.

Anyway, the constant wind was a problem, and many a time we had our cold weather hats blown off our heads only to watch them disappear into cloud. In my capacity as cold weather clothing man, I contacted the stores in Port Stanley and asked that they send some more up for us. Although Port Stanley was not too far away, their weather was completely different to ours. We were in warm arctic gear and they walked around with shirt sleeves rolled up. The storeman I spoke to was as helpful as ever. He advised me that the weather was not bad enough for arctic kit and that I would have to go without. I complained up the line until I was talking to the junior officer in charge of stores. In the end, I invited him up to Mount Kent to see what we were faced with. I arranged for him to arrive by the first flight of the day and leave by the last. That should give him enough time to suffer mild hypothermia, I thought. Sure enough, he arrived in his clean, but totally inadequate uniform. I gave him the usual site tour, but took my time outside. I apologized that I had no spare cold weather clothing to offer him for the duration of his visit. He got the message and true to his word (albeit given through chattering teeth), the first flight of the following day brought us our much needed replacement arctic clothing.

Despite the bad weather, we had about three days of sunshine during my whole time on the mountain. A couple of the Army lads decided that they wanted to try and get a sun tan. Working on the principle that the air was thinner on Mount Kent than at normal sea level, they thought that they would tan in no time. Suntan lotion was not readily available on the top of a mountain, so to speed up the process of tanning, one of them came up with the bright idea of smothering themselves in cooking oil. Some seven or so hours later, two extremely burnt soldiers presented themselves to me hoping that I would put them out of their misery. I wanted to send them to Port Stanley as they were quite badly burned, but they told me that if I did that, they would get charged for self-inflicted wounds. I covered them in special burn cream, wrapped them in bandages and redressed their burns every four hours. Their Sergeant found out about it and made them both run up and down the mountain carrying one of the missiles as a punishment. They must have been in agony but completed the task anyway. To top it all, neither of them got a tan!

It was quite a treat to get off the mountain, and one day I had to go to Stanley to collect some medical equipment. Whenever anyone escaped for the day, we put a notice on the wall in the Puffin Club and others would write a sort of shopping list. The items would be purchased and handed out in the bar later that evening. Usual items included cigarettes, shaving items and chocolate. I returned from the trip with all goods requested and arrived at the Bar like Father Christmas with his sack of goodies. The evening was run like an award ceremony with 'winners' being invited to collect their prize. All good fun. One Army lad had asked for a comb, and I had hunted high and low until, yes even in the Falklands, I managed to find a large pink comb. That met with roars of approval from all his mates. My final shopping triumph was saved until last, when one of the other Army lads had written "20 Embassy fags. If they haven't got them – anything". As he came to get his 'prize' I told him that they didn't have his fags and gave him an apple. He just stood there staring at the apple, while everyone else fell about. He must have been on freeze frame for a good few minutes, standing there in total disbelief, until I gave in and threw his fags at him.

My next time off the mountain was not such a success. From the mountain site, I could see Estancia Creek away to the North West. It looked a beautiful place. Again, hard to imagine what it was like on the night 3 Para liberated it from the Argentine soldiers. My plan was to set off early one morning, walk to Estancia, spend a few hours fishing, and walk back up the mountain. Sounded easy at the time! After all it only looked about two miles away. The small group of intrepid fishermen left the Mountain at six o'clock in the morning, finally arriving at Estancia Creek at about 11 o'clock! The small rolling hills we could see from the mountaintop turned out to be an endless chain of *large* rolling hills. I was shattered even before we arrived at the creek. My admiration and respect for those who were here in 1982 grew considerably. I was in no state to fish, let alone fight a battle. That said, I soon found out that I wouldn't have to fish either, as we had taken so long getting to our destination that the tide had gone out! A few military curses later, it was decided not to waste the day out, so a large fire was started, using wood left by the tide and large handfuls of heather. All food carried was soon disposed of before it was time to put out the fire and begin the long slog home. Unfortunately for us, it was now mostly uphill. Several hours later, we were back on the mountain site and being abused by all over the fact that we had missed the tide. At that point I was too tired to care. That had been the most walking I had done in about two months. I slept well that night!

Mount Kent used to encourage visitors as it gave us a new face to talk to, and it also let others on the Islands see how our facility worked. One of the many visitors was a young, female Army nurse from the hospital at Stanley. The day of her visit coincided with the weekly Chinook container run and someone in their wisdom decided that she could help attach one of the three container slings to the underside of the helicopter. This job is known as 'hooking' and can be quite dangerous. It requires you to kneel on the top of whatever is being collected by the helicopter, raising a heavy chain and loop, and hooking it onto one of the three hooks which hang from the underside of the helicopter, which is usually hovering no more than two or three feet above your head. As usual, our visitor was inadequately dressed for the climate we endured, so she was loaned a jacket which was slightly too large for her. Hard hat and goggles donned, she was positioned in the middle of the roof of the container that was about to be collected. The Chinook rose up the mountainside and was positioned over the top of the container before starting its slow descent. At the appropriate height it was held in the hover and the skill of the pilots was challenged by the strong cross wind. The two regular 'hookers' had attached the front and rear slings without any trouble. Our visitor was struggling a bit with the weight of the chain. The front 'hooker' turned to face the nurse and took her chain in order to help attach it to the helicopter. Unfortunately, once the weight of the chain had been taken from the nurse, the immense downdraft of the helicopters rotors caused her oversized jacket to inflate like a balloon, and she was flung off the container. Our inflatable nurse was last seen disappearing off the edge of the container collection area and bouncing down the mountainside. Amid the applause and cheering of all who had seen the spectacular event, I set off after her, fully expecting to follow a trail of nurse bits, but to her credit she remained in one piece and was, to my amazement, tearful but undamaged. I believe that she was the only person, not stationed on the mountain, to get the much-prized catwalk diving certificate, the award issued to anyone blown off the top of the mountain.

Other visitors included the monthly Combined Services Entertainment shows. These were up and coming entertainers who were booked to tour the Islands, performing for all the troops. On the whole they were OK and were welcome breaks from the routine. On one occasion, Charlie Chester toured the Islands. I was interviewed for his BBC Radio Two show and managed to get The Beatles record Ask Me Why played for Pauline, who was coping very well with the separation and being pregnant. A memorable visitor was a young woman employed by the NAAFI to tour all outlying sites and set up a barber shop. You could always recognize those from outlying sites, as they resembled yetis. Someone in Headquarters must have got themselves upset by the thought of long haired military men and employed this girl to sort out the undisciplined rabble. She flew onto Mount Kent one morning and was staying until the following day. That would give her enough time to cut seventy heads of hair. Accommodation was made available to her and she set about her hairdressing for the day. One of the civilian contractors took a shine to her and went back to have his hair cut three times! In the evening it would be safe to say that our 'guest' did not have to buy one drink in the Puffin Club. No problems so far. However, the bar closed and everyone drifted back to their accommodation. I was woken at about one o'clock in the morning by someone hammering on the medical centre door. Bleary eyed, I stumbled out of bed and answer the door. One of the civilian contractors is standing there with his mate (the one who took a shine to the hairdresser). I can't help but notice the large gaping cut along the chin of this extremely drunken Romeo. Blood was dripping all over my clean floor! Apparently, he had fancied his chances and staggered across to where the young lady was accommodated. He forgot about the cut down 40 gallon oil drum filled with water, which is used, like a swimming pool foot bath, to wash boots prior to going inside the living areas. On approaching the door to try his chances, he tripped and fell, banging his chin on the edge of the oil drum. Good cut though, with loads of claret. Romeo is invited in and told to lie on the examination couch whilst I struggle to wake myself up. The pain must have started to register as he started to become somewhat abusive towards me. As if it had been my fault! I told him to shut up and readied the suture kit. The insults continued along the lines of me being a 'mincer' and a 'puff', because I was doing a woman's job. Not a clever thing to say when you're at the wrong end of something sharp. Having dropped two needles on the floor because I was not fully awake, I successfully closed the wound with the third needle. All the time there was a barrage of abuse, even though his friend who had brought him to me was telling him to shut up. I had had enough. Some time earlier I had found a large yellow button. I remembered where it was and thought now would be a good time to give it a new home. I gave it a good wash and 'tagged' it to one of the sutures holding Romeo's chin together. Fortunately he was too drunk to realise what was going on and his friend though that he deserved what he got. Once I had finished, Romeo's friend took him away and I went back to bed feeling somewhat pleased with myself. The plan was to take the button off in the morning after he had apologized to me.

Half past seven the following morning I thought that the medical centre door was about to come off its hinges. I opened the door and was not surprised to see Romeo stood there. He was a sorry sight. Small red sunken eyes sitting in the middle of a very pale face. He looked like he had the hangover from hell itself. Oh, and he had a big yellow button sewn on to his chin! He started to give me a bit of grief so I reminded him that that was why he had ended up the way he had, and that an apology for his conduct may be a better course of action. I didn't tell him that I could take the button off at any time and said the stitches would have to stay in place for between seven and ten days. He stormed off. I saw him a little later, walking around with a scarf covering his lower face, however his friend had told everyone about my little deed and it soon became common knowledge. I left the button on for two days before taking it off his chin. Lesson learnt and message sent to all about messing with the one person who was there to look after them. In all, fortunately I had very few serious problems to deal with and it was more of a preventative role for me.

Christmas and New Year came and went and it was soon time for me to leave Mount Kent and return home. I was to be taken off the mountain a week before I was due to fly home in order to give me time to (I presume) return to some sort of normality. I protested and asked that I be allowed to stay on the mountain until the day before I was due to fly home. However that was not to be and I spent a week in Port Stanley. I have to admit to feeling quite sad at leaving, especially as most of the guys turned out to wave me off. Once back on the floating hotel, I had a walk around Stanley, visiting the Cathedral I had seen on my flight out to Mount Kent, and also the large monument in honour of those who fell during the conflict. Like the fallen of all wars before them, they too should not be forgotten and every Remembrance Sunday my mind casts back to standing in front of the memorial.

The week soon passed and I was stood in the departure lounge of Stanley Airfield, waiting for my flight home. The RAF had taken over from British Airways and now undertook the flights to and from the Falklands, using Tristar aeroplanes. Roles reversed from four months ago, I was now one of the excited faces looking at the depressed passengers arriving on the Islands. A large cheer went up as the Tristar left the runway and banked right in a steep climb. I would be home in about sixteen hours.

Chapter 6

After two weeks annual leave, I returned to work at RAF Staxton Wold (Driffield). Little had changed and apart from boring Gordon with the war stories, we carried on where we had left off - trying to set each other up with different practical jokes. I was also back to square one with regards sorting out the medical centre. There had been a succession of medics looking after the place for me and none had been too keen in keeping everything up to date. Yet again, medical documents were missing and medical appointments were overdue. I had an interesting time when, following a routine medical examination of the Station Commander, I instigated a specialist appointment as the CO was found to be slightly deaf in one ear. Nothing that would affect his everyday life, but enough to require his medical employment standard to be altered slightly. Under normal circumstances, this is little else than an administrative exercise for medical staff, and a regular review with the specialist for the patient. However, it caused a bit of a stir because everyone seemed to think that it would have huge career affecting implications for the Wing Commander. I was duly summoned to various Squadron and Flight Commanders and asked if I could simply overlook the findings or find an alternative way of dealing with the situation. I don't think it was the fact that I refused that annoyed them, more that I refused to even talk to them about it. I am a great believer in confidentiality and as the CO's medical history had nothing to do with them I refused to discuss it. The CO accepted the inevitable after I had explained everything fully to him and advised him that no matter how much pressure was applied to me, I would do my job. Life was uncomfortable for a few months afterwards, but not unbearable. I had more important things to worry about because Pauline was now over seven months pregnant and the baby would soon make his appearance.

All Station Commanders conduct regular inspections of departments on their station and I was dreading my next one purely because of the issue regarding his medical category. He duly arrived, began the usual tour and asked all the usual questions. He was nothing but professional and my opinion of him increased. The inspection entourage included the Station Warrant Officer (to do the shouting when below standard things were found), Officer Commanding the Administration Wing (my line manager) and an admin clerk to do the writing. I knew and liked the admin clerk and we would mutter and complain as we followed the inspection team around the building. As we walked into one of the offices, the clerk muttered to me, "You jammy sod. I'll bet you're really pleased."
I thought he was talking about the fact that I was soon to be a dad, and agreed with him, practicing the soon to be used new father 'Cheshire Cat' grin. He continued, "I'll

bet you're wife's pleased too. What will you do with your house?"

"Well I've already decorated the nursery, and she'll be glad when it's all over and done with." At that point he gave me a puzzled look and said,

"I'm on about your posting, what are you on about?" I had absolutely no idea that I was to be posted and asked where I was going. I began to think that this was typical of the RAF, as at the most inappropriate point of your life, they would always conjure up another little trick to mess you about.

"Where am I going, and more importantly, when?" I asked my friend. He was looking very uncomfortable and said he couldn't tell me as the CO wanted to drop the bombshell on me at the end of the inspection. I couldn't wait. I needed to know now and pestered him constantly. He gave in but made me promise to act surprised when I was formally told.

"Where in the world would you least like to go?"

"Scotland." was my immediate reply.

"Where in the world would you most like to go?"

I thought a little, remembering that I had applied to serve overseas in Cyprus, Gibraltar or Hong Kong.

"Cyprus." I replied, because I knew the other two were such exclusive postings that I wouldn't stand a chance.

"No mate, you're off to Sek Kong, you jammy sod!"

I couldn't believe it. We were going to Hong Kong. I have to say that I remember little else about the inspection and that, true to my word, I acted very surprised when the CO proudly announced that I was to be posted. It was, however, quite short notice. I had two and a half months before leaving. In that time, I had to not only become the proud father to Mark, but fit in a month long Aeromedical Evacuation course at RAF Brize Norton. Not to worry, the hassle of such a short time scale would be worth the result.

I had planned to go home that night and pretend to be really annoyed with the RAF at posting me. I was going to ham it up for Pauline. However, I was so excited at the prospect of going to Hong Kong that within an hour of the Station Commander leaving the building, I was on the telephone. Pauline was quite excited, but like me, a little concerned about the immediate future.

I was soon off to RAF Brize Norton for the four-week course in Aeromedical Evacuation. The first two weeks in the classroom and the final two weeks spent on actual flights. During the classroom phase, we had to learn about eight different airframes, from Puma helicopters up to the Tristar airliner. On the final test, we were presented with line drawings of all the airframes, on which we had to mark the locations of safety equipment such as fire extinguishers, all emergency exits and fire axes. We also had to know the location of all stretcher fitting points and communication and power sockets. In all, a busy two weeks! The reward at the end was two actual flights during which, our instructors would assess our performance. Prior to the flights, we had to write and send all the signals, select and pack all medical kit, stretchers and harnesses, and anything else we may require for the trip. My trips were to the Falklands and to Germany. I'd only been back a month and a half and I was to fly back to the damn Falklands! It was a flight from hell last time.

God knows what it was going to be like under assessment and with patients. I wasn't disappointed. It was still hell.

The only benefits were that all aeromed team members were treated as flight crew. Our meals were served on a proper tray as opposed to those horrible plastic trays you get when flying on holiday. To the rear of the aircraft were numerous empty seats so I found a bank of four together, took a blanket out of the medical kit, stretched out and went to sleep. Mount Pleasant airfield was still being built so the Tristar had to land on the short runway at Stanley. I was lucky enough to be allowed to stand behind the pilot as we touched down. A very impressive display of skill on his part. The wind was gusting and the approach appeared to be quite challenging. Once off the aircraft, we were taken to our respective accommodation blocks, with arrangements to meet at the Medical Centre a few hours later. Arrangements had been made for us to see the patients due to return with us in one week's time. Once that had been completed, the time was our own until the day before we were all due to fly back, unless there were any complications or further patients to be flown home. I tried to arrange a trip back up to Mount Kent, but unfortunately this was not to be so.

All my patients for this trip were walking wounded which made it a little easier with regard checking them through immigration and getting them settled on the aircraft. I was being assessed on the flight between the Falklands and the Ascension Islands. After that, another team took over and I could retire to the back of the aircraft to have another sleep. It was a very easy flight with no problems from either the patients of the assessing staff. I was relieved to get back to the UK as it was getting closer and closer to the date that the baby was due. I didn't want to be nine thousand miles away when Pauline went into labour.

My other check flight was a trip to Germany. This time we were due to fly back on an Andover aircraft, which was a small propeller driven aircraft. Again, I was lucky as all my patients were walking wounded. In fact, the majority of them were recovering alcoholics. An unfortunate side effect of the cheap German beer! Fortunately for me, they were not allowed to bring any duty free alcohol back with them. Due to the fact that I would soon be "wetting the baby's head" I managed to bring back a few extra crates of beer and write them off against names of patients on the flight. Unfortunately for me, my few extra crates, stacked on the back ramp of the Andover, upset the balance of the aircraft and the loadmaster had to rearrange some of the other cargo. It was very kind of him, as he would have been well within his rights to tell me to leave the beer behind. Fortunately, the captain of the aircraft never found out. I believe he was told that we had to carry a lot of medical equipment. The best about it was that I had passed the course and finished in time to be present at the birth of our son, Mark. With mother and baby fine, I wanted for nothing. However, after seven weeks I had to leave them and fly to Hong Kong alone, as there were no married quarters available straight away. It was seven weeks before a flat was to become available, and arrangements were made for Pauline and Mark to fly out.

Until a flat became available, I lived in multiple occupancy single accommodation with three other guys. It was like joining the RAF all over again. The camaraderie on the station was excellent. There were frequent organized events and trips around Hong Kong. I enjoyed going to them, but missed being with Pauline and Mark. Eventually, I was told that a flat had become available and I was given a date that I could take it over. Finally we could settle down as a family. I was looking forward to their arrival, although I had to tell Pauline that within a week of her arrival, I was to fly back to the UK for a week on what was called a reverse Aeromed. My patient was a Gurkha soldier who was suspected of suffering epilepsy. Pauline was not too happy but accepted the inevitable. I felt terrible leaving her with a newborn baby in a foreign country. However, the week in the UK soon passed and we all settled into the life of expatriates.

Hong Kong was fantastic. As a family we settled into the lifestyle very quickly. However the continual hustle and bustle took a little getting used to. The Medical Centre was a combined RAF and Army establishment with a contingent of Hong Kong Service Corps personnel. There were also Chinese and Gurkha nurses working there. Quite the United Nations! I was fortunate that I had worked with the Army before, as it takes some getting used to. Duties as the duty medic came around about once a week with a duty weekend about every five to six weeks. I didn't mind them too much but was always a little short with people who, in my opinion, were presenting themselves out of hours for non-emergency type complaints. We were not supposed to sleep when on duty, but if there were no in-patients, I sometimes had a sleep on the sofa in the rest room. It was very uncomfortable so I usually just dozed.

One night there was a knock on the door and I walked the length of the corridor to be confronted with the sight of a Gurkha standing there holding a small plastic bag.

"Can I help you?" I politely asked. His reply was that a centipede had bitten him. I wasn't very pleased and began to remonstrate to him my displeasure. He was very apologetic and somewhat reluctantly offered me his plastic bag, saying that he had captured this monster which had so savagely attacked him. I took the bag and looked inside, almost jumping out of my skin as the largest centipede I had ever seen nonchalantly gazed up at me as if to say "What are you looking at?"

I would say that it was about six inches in length and about a quarter of an inch thick. At the front was a set of magnificent pincer like jaws. I immediately invited the soldier in and asked him to lie down on the examination couch. Without him looking I tied the top of the plastic bag and left the savage beast outside. Upon examining the soldier I became aware of severe, angry red swelling tracking, before my very eyes, up his arm. A degree in rocket science was not needed to realise that he was suffering a severe allergic reaction to the bite and that I would have to be quick in treating him. A phone call to the duty doctor was made and treatment in the form of an anti-histamine injection was given. We kept the Gurkha soldier in the medical centre for the remainder of the night and thankfully he recovered enough to return to work the following morning. What he didn't know was that I had crept back outside the Medical Centre and battered the plastic bag, complete with centipede against the wall until I considered it safe enough for me to go back inside. I didn't feel very brave, but I felt safe.

That wasn't my only encounter with some of the more exotic forms of Hong Kong wildlife. Another night, some months later, I was again on duty when the doorbell rang in the early hours of the morning. I went to the front door to be faced with the sight of another Gurkha soldier holding his head, screaming something about being possessed and headbutting the walls on either side of the entrance porch. Nervously, I opened the door and through the half-inch or so gap, I tried to ask what the problem was. He continued to shout and was slapping the side of his head with his hand. I reluctantly let this apparent madman into the Medical Centre and began to take him down to the treatment room. Walking down the corridor, he started shaking his head again and zigzagged between the corridor walls headbutting them as he went. I have to say the whole experience was somewhat unnerving. Eventually, we reached the treatment room and I managed to get him to sit in a chair so that I could try to work out what on Earth was going on. He kept banging his head and pointing to his ear so I thought I'd better have a look into his ear canal. I placed a plastic trumpet on the end of an aurescope and placed him in a half head lock so as to keep his head as still as possible before placing the plastic cone shaped trumpet into his ear canal. I'm sure I visibly jumped as when I looked through the magnifying lens and down the illuminated trumpet, I came face to face with the back end of a large moth. The moth was still alive and not too happy about its immediate predicament. It was frantically flapping its tiny wings in an attempt to extract itself from the tiny space it had accidentally flown into. Apparently the poor Gurkha had been out on a night time exercise, walking through some long grass when along flew the moth on a trajectory, which placed it on an exact collision course with a passing Nepalese ear canal. The instantaneous noise must have been horrendous! An instruction had been issued by the doctors that no medics were to insert surgical instruments (or anything else for that matter) into ear canals. Whatever the problem, the duty doctor was to be called. I made an instant decision that this poor soldier was going to go mad in the very near future if I did not do something to alleviate his problem. I poured some warm olive oil into his ear in the hope that it would deaden some of the noise and eventually drown the insect. Unfortunately, the moth had other ideas and went ballistic. The flapping of the wings caused most of the olive oil to be sprayed back out. The Gurkha was getting quite distressed. I took a set of sterile ear forceps and carefully took hold of the back of the moth. Pulling gently the moth came out. The Gurkha immediately settled while the moth continued to show its displeasure. I was about to give it the same treatment as the centipede from a few months earlier, when the Gurkha told me not to kill it. He asked for it to be put in a specimen jar so that he could take it away to show his friends! How could I refuse? Now he was calm, I called the duty doctor so that he could have a check of the ear to make sure there was no damage and prescribe antibiotic cover. He was very good about my decision to remove the moth and I did not get into trouble.

On other occasions I was not so tolerant. A Chinese fireman presented himself at something like 2 O'clock in the morning. As usual, I had been having a crafty sleep on the old sofa and had tried to look as awake as possible before reaching the front door. The fireman was casually leaning on the wall of the entrance looking in the pink of health. When I asked him what was wrong, he made out that he could not speak any English. I knew that he would probably speak a little as he worked on the airfield and would have to be able to speak with the air traffic controllers. However, on this occasion he chose not to. I again asked him what the problem was and he stood up off the wall and rubbed the top of his head with his fingertips. I told him that I didn't understand and asked if he had banged his head. Again, he rubbed his fingertips on his head. I told him again that I didn't understand him. At that point he brought from his trouser pocket a bottle of medicated shampoo. He shook the bottle to show me that it was empty and rubbed his head again. I took the bottle from him and made out that the light had finally dawned for me as I asked if he just wanted a new bottle of shampoo. Suddenly being able to speak English, his face lit up as he nodded the affirmative. I was less than pleased at having been disturbed in the early hours of the morning by someone with nocturnal dandruff. I threw the empty bottle across the car park and pushed the fireman out of the doorway. I was teaching him some new English words as I chased him across the car park and off into the darkness. So much for the caring profession.

There were times when proper emergencies required a more professional approach. A Gurkha mother brought in her young child who was lapsing in and out of consciousness. After a quick examination by one of the doctors, a decision was made to fly the boy to the British Military Hospital in Kowloon. Driving in Hong Kong was a nightmare due to the volume of traffic. By road, on average, the journey took in the region of two hours. A helicopter was scrambled and I duly took the four or five year old on board. Apparently he had been playing on a compost heap and had eaten a root type plant before becoming ill. Mother was strapped next to me and I kept the boy under observation. During the fifteen-minute flight, he lapsed into unconsciousness again. The noise and vibration of a helicopter makes it very difficult to assess patient's vital signs so I took off my flying helmet and held my face next to the boy's, to see if he was still breathing. Fortunately he was, but I was getting very concerned about him. He was extremely pale, unresponsive and very limp. We soon arrived in the usual rugby field to the rear of the hospital and I was relieved to see the ambulance waiting for us to land. I don't know why I was relieved, as the ambulance had never let us down before. With mother and child safely transferred to the ambulance crew, I sat back in the helicopter and enjoyed the flight back to Sek Kong. I telephoned the hospital a few days later to see how the little boy was doing and was told that he would make a full recovery. I was also asked the question "Did you know that he had tuberculosis?"

I hadn't, and now became a little concerned that my face had been little more than 3-4 inches from his face for most of the flight. I spoke to the Squadron Leader doctor and told him that my last patient had tuberculosis and what would he like me to do. He was very laid back and told me not to worry. I was to 'give him a shout' if I developed a cough. Great. That said, Squadron Leader Don Woods was a good doctor. I don't think I ever saw him in a state of panic over anything.

Such was his relaxed attitude, when I went to see him about getting a medical examination prior to undertaking my first parachute course, he asked me if I felt well and duly signed my form when I replied that I did! The whole consultation took place when we passed in the corridor of the medical centre and lasted about 30 seconds. I thoroughly enjoyed my parachute jump but was a little surprised when I looked down after the successful deployment of my parachute to see rice fields everywhere instead of the airfield. The jumpmaster, the person who tells you when to actually jump from the aeroplane, had told us to jump too early. Still, there was little I could do about it. I couldn't just climb back on board. I turned towards the airfield and just about made it back inside of the perimeter fence. I landed safely, right next to the female accommodation block with my parachute unceremoniously draped over the lamppost to the front of the block. I wanted to continue parachuting, but never actually got around to it.

The only other brush I had with the parachuting world was when the emergency telephone rang one lunchtime. An excited voice told me that there had been a parachuting accident and that someone's parachute had failed to open. A scout helicopter was on its way to the Medical Centre to collect medical staff. The only other person in the building was Squadron Leader Woods. He just said that I could go if I wanted to and left it at that. Right then, that'll be me going, I thought. I climbed into my flying kit and collected the medical equipment I thought I would need. Just at that point I heard the sound of the helicopter approaching. I had visions of having to run across the car park and jumping aboard. Not so. As I left the front door of the Medical Centre, the helicopter was completing a steep, fast landing in the car park itself. The skids scuffed the tarmac as the helicopter came to an abrupt halt. Fantastic flying by the pilot. The car park wasn't exactly the largest of areas and was square in shape at the end of a short road. As I left the front door, to my right was St Martin's Church and to my left was the NAFFI shop. With it being lunchtime, the NAFFI was packed. Everyone had come out to see what was happening as it was unusual, to say the least, to see a helicopter land in this area. I raised my thumb to the pilot to get his permission to approach the aircraft. He returned the thumbs up and I ran towards the open door, leaning forward so as not to get too close to the turning rotor blades not too far above my head. I threw my medical kit on board and stood on the skid, trying to plug in my helmet intercom so that I could get the latest information on the parachutist. As I was doing this, the pilot began to lift the helicopter off the ground. I had yet to strap myself into the harness. Frantically plugging in the intercom I shouted at the pilot that I was not secured. He laughed and told me to make sure that I had a good grip on the doorframe. At this point of sheer panic I looked back at the car park to see all the people from the NAFFI, standing on the grass outside, looking up at the helicopter. I don't know what possessed me but I started waving like some demented hero or departing American President. It probably looked quite cool from the ground, but at that point it would have taken a crowbar to prise my fingers off the doorframe.

Out of sight of the crowd, I hurriedly climbed inside and waited for us to arrive at the landing zone used by the parachutists. A short flight later, we landed in the field that had been used as the landing zone for the day. I made my way to a small huddle of people who appeared to be surrounding someone. I had visions of finding an individual who resembled a concertina and would only require for me to diagnose death and wait the arrival of a doctor to formally certify. Fortunately I was very surprised. The poor bloke was very conscious and in a lot of pain. His ankle was badly broken; so much so that I could see the bone sticking out through the skin and his foot was at a grotesque angle. There was little bleeding but I was still concerned enough to put a drip in him. My priority was to stabilize the fracture and to get him to hospital as soon as possible. Drip in place, I then gave him entonox to breath whilst I very gently applied tension to his foot and secured it in an inflatable splint. All the time this was going on, his friends from the parachute club kept pestering him for, of all things, a photograph. The poor sod was lying on the floor in agony and all his friends could say was "Smile." before pressing the shutter. The trip to the hospital would only take about 20 minutes by air so I was no too concerned. Once the patient was ready to move he was placed on a stretcher and flown to the hospital. Again we were met at the rugby pitch by the ambulance, and off he went. The parachute club later presented me with a set of the photographs as a momento of the day. It would be many months, but the parachutist made a full recovery.

There were several Gurkha Regiments in Hong Kong at any one time, and there was a healthy rivalry between them. Their downfall was that they had junior British officers posted to their Regiments. These young men had recently graduated from Sandhurst and had arrived to be placed in command of one of the most loyal and obedient group of soldiers ever recruited. The power sometimes clouded their judgement. One such incident was when one of the Gurkha Regiments set off to complete their annual combat fitness test. This required the regiment as a whole to march a distance of eight miles in approximately one hour and ten minutes. Each soldier had to complete the march in what is known as 'fighting order'. That means carrying equipment on a webbing belt that had to weigh at least 35 pounds, in addition to each soldier carrying his rifle and kevlar helmet. One lunchtime in the medical centre, a Gurkha soldier rushed in to tell us that about fifteen of his regiment were being brought in suffering from heat exhaustion. Also in the building was the RAF Nursing Officer Squadron Leader Evelyn Peters. I had never been particularly fond of, or complimentary of, RAF nurses, however there is always an exception to every rule, and Evelyn Peters was it. She was a very skilled practitioner and I was relieved that she was in the building. We looked at each other, thinking that we had heard the number of casualties wrongly and reconfirmed the information. When we were told that there was, in fact, sixteen casualties coming in we set about recalling other medics from lunch. Soon after, we had a conveyer belt reception waiting for the soldiers. On arrival each was assessed for priority of treatment. Those still able to look after themselves were stripped to underclothes and given cool water to sip. A medic remained with them constantly monitoring their progress. Those less able to look after themselves were brought through to where we waited. All the building fans had been set up in the treatment area and we had bed sheets sitting in buckets of cool water. When treating heat related illnesses, you have to be careful that you do not cool the casualty too quickly or you complicate matters and give yourself, and the casualty, more problems. The cooling process had to be carried out in a controlled way. Those who really had problems were brought in by stretcher and the first medic set about removing the clothing. While this was going on, another soldier was tasked with obtaining the name of the casualty and placing a wristband on them. Once stripped, the casualty was moved down the line to be cannulated, which is to have the needle inserted into the arm ready to accept the rehydrating fluid. It was my job to insert the cannula. I found it very easy as most heat illness casualties have veins like drainpipes as the body expands all blood vessels close to the skin, in an attempt to cool the blood. Once I had inserted the needle they were passed down the line to Evelyn Peters, who connected the bags of fluid and set them off dripping. The casualties were then passed to another medic who took them to the main ward for observation and assessment by the doctor. Apparently what had gone wrong on this particular fitness test was the junior officer of the regiment had decided to see how far his soldiers could go without drinking any of the water in their water bottles. He also chose to complete the test during midday, the hottest part of the day. Clever chap.

He made the mistake of turning up in the treatment area as his soldiers were being passed through. He was obviously inwardly panicking and trying to make amends for his stupidity but all he was succeeding in doing was getting in the way. He asked if there was anything he could do so I told him that he had done more than enough and maybe he would like to go away. He was about to turn all officer-like and go on about my insubordination when Evelyn suggested he left. As she outranked him by three ranks he decided to withdraw. She did tell me off later though. Once all the soldiers had been seen, the doctor decided that the most serious of the cases should be flown to hospital for urgent admission. Evelyn and I would escort him on the flight. All was going well on the flight until the soldier decided to have a heat induced fit. Not a good idea in the confined space of a Wessex Helicopter. There was little anyone could do to cool him further, as he already had a drip pouring fluid into him and the door of the helicopter had been left open to encourage a draft. We were carrying spare bottles of drip fluid in case we had to replace the one already running so Evelyn opened one and set about hosing the soldier down. Unorthodox, but very effective. The soldier soon stopped fitting and the remainder of the journey was uneventful.

I never really settled with the Army as they had a totally different way of working to those of us in the RAF. There was always that little bit of resentment about the RAF medics getting all the aeromed jobs too. Unfortunately, because we were working from an Army Medical Centre, we used to get caught up in their inspections and other forms of Army life. One day we had to all parade for an inspection by the Colonel. The formal tropical dress for the RAF consisted of khaki trousers and tunic. Most of the time we wore short sleeve shirts, shorts which ended just above the knees and knee length socks. Footwear was in the form of locally made desert boots. On this particular day I had had enough of the Army way of life and decided to make my own little protest. I wore my desert boots, instead of my highly polished boots, with my best uniform. We formed up ready to march on to the inspection area, which in reality was a corner of the car park at the front of the building. Everyone's shiny boots were crunching away as we marched on. There was no sound coming from my boots. We formed up and had the usual pre-inspection inspection by the Staff Sergeant. He stood in front of me working his way down from head to toe. As his eyes reached the floor I swear he swayed. After a few seconds of no more movement he looked at me, and in a very calm voice asked what the hell did I have on my feet. I pointed out the obvious to which he then exploded. He threw me off the parade screaming at how he was going to kill me when the inspection was over. He never did and I was more than happy with my little moral victory. RAF 1 – Army 0.

I was lucky to undertake several aeromedical flights out of Hong Kong. Brunei is a small oil-rich kingdom in Southeast Asia. Facing the South China Sea, and North of Borneo, it is a small but beautiful country. There is a small military presence there whose primary task is to train service personnel in jungle warfare and survival. This presence goes by the name of BATT, which stands for British Army Training Team. The senior person in charge is from the SAS.

My first aeromed there was to collect a 19 year old Royal Marine who had been involved in a boating accident. He had been 'on point' (at the front) of a longboat patrolling the rivers through the jungle. He had somehow fallen overboard and the boat had, in effect, run over him. The propeller on the outboard motor had badly damaged one of his legs and completely removed the other. By all accounts, the medics on duty at the scene had performed miracles and saved the young lad's life. By the time I got there he was stable and ready to fly to Hong Kong with me. I was well looked after by his mates in 45 Commando during my week long stay! I was taken into the jungle, which was only about a fifteen-minute walk from the camp. Quite weird really. One minute you were walking down the road, the next you were in dense jungle. These guys were in the jungle for weeks on end. I went in for one day and found it a quite oppressive place. Goodness knows how they managed! My other trip to Brunei was to collect a Gurkha soldier, who was suffering from really bad headaches. However, on the day we were due to fly back to Hong Kong, I began to have severe stomach cramps, along with nausea and vomiting. It's fair to say that my patient looked after me a lot better than I looked after him! Talk about role reversal!!

Another memorable trip was to Nepal, to collect a young Gurkha suffering from Guillan-Barre Syndrome. This is where the whole central nervous system is attacked by a virus, and results in what can only be described as a central nervous system shutdown. Apart from being able to breathe, he was paralysed. Unlike my solo trips to Brunei, I would be making this trip with Evelyn Peters.

We flew from Hong Kong a few hours before a Tropical Storm hit the colony. The dark grey clouds were approaching and could be seen clearly from the aircraft window as we climbed away from Kai Tak Airport. I felt guilty about leaving Pauline and Mark to the mercy of the horrible weather, with its high winds and driving rain. Hopefully it wouldn't be too bad and would blow itself out quite quickly. Landing in Kathmandu several hours later, Evelyn and I made our way out of the airport to be met by a member of the British Consulate. He took us to the hotel that we would use for our overnight stop, prior to flying on to Biratnagar in South East Nepal, close to the Nepalese and Indian border. We would be there for the week, catching a RAF VC10 flight back to Hong Kong.

Nepal is a beautiful country, but extremely poor. I had never seen such poverty first-hand and it quite shocked me. However, there was a great pride amongst the people. I remember asking a tailor for his permission to take his photograph. He smartened himself up, fastened all but the top button of his shirt, sat bolt upright and smiled. I got the impression that it was the most important thing that had happened to him in ages. A whistle stop tour of the beautiful city of Kathmandu was completed and, the following morning, Evelyn and I flew on to the British Army Hospital in Biratnagar. Our patient was as well as could be expected under the circumstances so there was little for us to do in the days leading up to flying back with him. Although I was a corporal, I was accommodated in the Sergeant's Mess. Along with that, I was allocated a 'batman'. I had great difficulty in coming to terms with that. No sooner had I stepped out of my uniform to go to the shower, my batman came along and whisked the clothing away only to return it later, immaculately cleaned and pressed. My shoes had not been so highly polished since Swinderby! I tried to make as little fuss for this chap as possible.

The week in this beautiful country passed all too quickly and the day of our return flight arrived. We were to catch an internal Nepalese flight to Kathmandu and meet up with the VC10 on the airfield the following morning. We would then load our stretcher bound patient onto the VC10 and fly back to Hong Kong. Simple! How wrong I was. The hospital transport took everyone to the airport in plenty of time for me to book Evelyn, myself and our patient through immigration. All these admin type tasks were mine as Evelyn's primary responsibility was the patient. We worked very well together as a team. All documentation completed, I returned to where I had left everybody to wait to board the aircraft. As we had a stretcher patient, we would board in the normal way – by using a catering truck with raised platform. We would also board before all the other passengers. However, half an hour before we were due to board, the problems began. The aircraft had a problem and would need an engineer to fly from Kathmandu in order to fix the problem. There would be a three hour delay a good chance that the flight would be cancelled for the day. We would miss our connection with the VC10.

As the small Britten Norman Islander aircraft, bringing the engineer approached, some hour and a half later, I had an idea. I asked Evelyn for some of her imprest money (money given to us prior to leaving so that we wouldn't have to use our own money). She looked a little puzzled but handed it over none the less. I wandered off and managed to find an airport official. I explained our predicament and made our patient sound as though he would die in the airport lounge if we didn't leave soon. I asked if there were any seats available on the Islander aircraft that had brought the engineer, as that was returning almost immediately. I said that I had a bit of cash and would be willing to pay for his permission. All highly illegal, but what Evelyn didn't know about, she couldn't worry about. The official looked interested in my proposal, so I palmed off some of the cash and handed it over. He looked at it and said that there was only enough cash for two seats. Greedy sod! I handed over a bit more of Her Majesty's cash and followed him in order to get our tickets. They were tickets for three seats, and our guy was a stretcher case! I took the tickets. It was this or nothing. I walked back to Evelyn and told her that we were leaving on the Islander and that we would have to prop our patient up between us. She nearly went purple! I made up some story about pleading with someone in the airport and that this was our only option so we should take it and sort out the finer points later. I didn't dare tell her that I'd bribed an official!

The flight from Biratnagar to Kathmandu was interesting to say the least. We took off and flew up and up, for what seemed ages. After that we flew off towards Kathmandu. It was only later that I found out that the compass had failed on the aircraft so the pilot decided to climb to a height where he could see Kathmandu and just fly towards it. During the flight, the cabin door began to rattle. The steward sat by the door and hung on to the handle to keep it quiet. Evelyn and I glanced towards each other on more than one occasion I can tell you! After what seemed an age, we landed in Kathmandu and we were again met by the British Consul chap. There was an ambulance there and it took us all back to the same hotel that we had stayed in on our first night. The patient and I would be sharing a room and I would need to turn him regularly through the night, as well as make sure he could get to the toilet whenever he needed. I wouldn't get much sleep, but I didn't mind. Like Evelyn, I always put my patients first.

The following morning arrived and we found ourselves at the airport waiting on the arrival of the VC10. After a few hours, we were all safely on board, waiting to make the last journey back to Hong Kong. It went without a hitch, and we handed over our patient to a British Army Nursing team on our arrival back in Hong Kong. Evelyn and I then returned back to RAF Sek Kong, replenished all medical kit and then took the rest of the day off to recover. I went to see the patient in the British Military Hospital on a few occasions and he was doing fine. As with all Gurkhas, he was an absolute gentleman who did not complain. He was always smiling and putting on a brave face. I was proud to have been able to help him.

However, as they say, all good things come to an end. It was soon time for us all to pack up and return to the UK. The two and a half years we spent in Hong Kong were fantastic. I was fortunate enough to visit Brunei twice and Nepal once. I was also lucky to survive a couple of incidents while flying; one where the helicopter engines failed when flying through the mountainous area and another when a helicopter window shattered and threw pieces of perspex all over my back. As a family we had had some great holidays, a number of visitors came to stay with us and we have many happy memories of our time in the Far East. I had thoroughly enjoyed my tour of duty. Mark was christened in Hong Kong and both Pauline and I were confirmed by the Bishop of Hong Kong. However, after a high, there is always a low. Someone in the RAF had a sense of humour when they decided that at the end of my tour, which was in December 1988, I was to be posted to RAF Kinloss in North Scotland. Talk about extremes of temperature. Still, all good things come to an end and it was with some sadness that we saw ourselves aboard our final flight from Kai Tak airport.

Chapter 7

My introduction to life in Scotland was interesting, to say the least. I had been allocated a married quarter and would be allowed to move in just before Christmas of 1989. My dad and I drove up to Kinloss on 19 December with a view to getting all the furniture delivered the following day. I accepted the quarter and dad and I set off to find the local pub for something to eat and a pint. We spent the night in sleeping bags on the floor of the living room, getting woken up every so often by the noise of the Nimrods taking off and landing.

The following morning we waited for the furniture to be delivered but, when nothing had arrived by lunchtime, I decided to phone up to see if I could get a delivery time. I was advised that our furniture had been impounded by HM Customs as they were unhappy with one item – my bicycle. Customs believed it to be new, and wanted to charge me import duty. I told them it was two years old and, if they removed the packaging, would find several areas of rust confirming my story. I was fuming. As a result of this, the furniture would not be delivered as planned. Dad and I could have gone back to Liverpool the previous day and been at home for my mum's birthday on the 20th. We decided to leave that afternoon and arrive back in Liverpool as a birthday surprise for my mum. I am so glad that we did. Driving back down that evening, dad and I stopped off at a garage to fill up and to buy a haggis as a birthday present for mum. We made if back and it was a lovely surprise for mum when we turned up on the doorstep.

The following day saw the terrible incident at Lockerbie. Dad was a little shaken when he showed me the petrol receipt from the day before. We had stopped at the little Lockerbie garage at, give or take 10 minutes, the same time as the accident, 24 hours earlier. Had the furniture been delivered as expected, we may well have been in Lockerbie at the time that Pan Am flight 103 came crashing down.

Just after Christmas, Pauline, Mark and I drove up to Kinloss to start our life up in Scotland. Our furniture had been released by Customs and would be delivered the day after our arrival. We drove back up through Lockerbie and saw, first hand, the ugly scar that ran through the small Scottish town. There was a huge elongated crater, several damaged houses and several pieces of the Boeing 747 still lying about. It is a sight I doubt I will forget in a long time.

I have to say that settling into life at RAF Kinloss in Scotland was more difficult than settling into life half way around the world in Hong Kong. Not only were we right at the top of the country, but I also found it difficult settling back into life with just the RAF and no Army to be seen. This would be the first time in four years that I would not be working with the Army. There was a good Flight Sergeant at RAF Kinloss who made me feel very welcome. His name was Nick Green. The RAF did the usual trick and told him that he would not be moving for several years and, after he bought a house in the local area, told him that he was to be promoted to Warrant Officer and posted to a unit in London. The man with the sense of humour had struck again!

RAF Kinloss was home to numbers 120, 201 and 206 Squadrons of Nimrod aircraft. The Nimrod is a derivative of the De Havilland Comet civilian airliner whose primary task is one of maritime patrol and search and rescue. Sadly for me, there were no helicopters. The station was situated on the North coast of Scotland, right on the Moray Firth. It was a fabulous location, but almost permanently cold and wet. Quite a shock, after Hong Kong. The Nimrod Squadrons primary tasks were to locate and co-ordinate the rescue of downed aircrew, or other persons in need of rescue and to patrol the shores of the United Kingdom looking for Soviet aircraft and submarines. The aircraft has the capability of both radar and sonar, with the aircrew operators being referred to as 'wet' or 'dry' depending on which equipment they worked on. Most of the time, however, they just ate food and the Nimrod was referred to as a flying galley! To watch a Nimrod being scrambled on a mission was impressive. If you were on duty, the station tannoy would announce "Dinghy, Dinghy, Dinghy. I say again, Dinghy, Dinghy, Dinghy". A few minutes later, you would hear the distinct sound of the engines winding up. A few minutes after that, you would hear the aircraft roar into the sky. If you were off duty, and walking along the road that passed the end of one of the runways, you could stand and watch as the hunter/killer Nimrod taxied at speed along the taxiway, before tuning onto the runway. It carried on rolling, the engine noise increased, and the aircraft hurtled down the runway before leaving RAF Kinloss behind in a trail of engine exhaust fumes. This was even more impressive if the Nimrod was taking off towards you as opposed to taking off away from you.

As the unit played a major part in the defence of the United Kingdom, a large part of our time was spent on exercise. They were usually a few days in length and, of course, we won each time. Most of our time on exercise was spent dealing with imaginary casualties who were brought to us in various states of simulated damage and our task was to prioritise their injuries and treat them accordingly. I think we were very successful, as even some of those casualties who were pronounced dead would turn up several hours or the following day later. They would invariably be asked, "Hey, didn't you die yesterday?" to which the bored reply was always "Yeah, but you did such a good job I thought I'd get a second opinion." Most of my time during exercises was spent at the front door of the Medical Reception area, as one of my roles was to carry out the triage of the casualties, and decide who was admitted first. Other medics then took the casualties into the treatment area where they were seen either by a doctor or, if the injuries were relatively minor, by other medics. It all became a little frantic if casualties were brought to us just after an air raid, as we had to assume that either chemical or biological agents had contaminated them.

All these casualties had to be decontaminated before they could be assessed and treated. The process was carried out with everybody in full chemical protective suits known as NBC or Noddy suits. It was hot, demanding work and I was usually nominated as team leader for this process. During any exercise, or if there really had been a conflict, the medical centre was relocated to a hardened hangar on the edge of the airfield. In peacetime it functioned as a sports area and was fully laid out with a five-a-side football pitch and a basketball court. One of the most important pieces of equipment taken with us on any exercise was a football. This almost led to the downfall of the medical empire on one exercise as during a prolonged air attack, when most casualties would be expected and everyone was supposed to be in full chemical warfare clothing, we had a surprise visit from the dreaded Distaff – Directing Staff who assessed the unit's performance as a whole. They were always identifiable by their white armband, ever-ready clipboard and miserable looking face. Imagine their surprise when they walked into the medical reception area, expecting to see a line of fully kitted medics eagerly awaiting the arrival of airmen and airwomen injured, maimed and killed in the line of duty. What they really found was most of the medical staff (including the doctors) half dressed and running around the five-a-side football pitch. Our NBC jackets were hanging in a long line over one of the pitch enclosing walls. We were supposed to be at war, so I suppose the only expression I could use was that the Distaff went ballistic. He immediately killed us all off as we were not wearing our respirators or full protective suits, but then immediately resurrected us, as without medical staff the unit could not function properly. After that, though, we were constantly bombarded with casualties and suspect bombs outside of the building.

I have to say that apart from the exercises, and the odd adventure, life at RAF Kinloss was very routine and boring. There was a Sergeant, Ivor Fuller, posted in not long after I arrived, and to say he was useless would be a compliment to him. He was the first person ever to fail the trade promotion course, only to be sent back again on the next one and scrape through by the skin of his teeth. It was common knowledge that he had only been given a good enough assessment so as to be considered for promotion, so that his last boss could get rid of him. Their gain, definitely our loss. One of his tricks, when he did not know what to do, was to give the problem to someone else under the cover of, "Here's a bit of trade training, have a go at sorting this out." When an individual suffered an injury or illness which took them below a fitness level which would reduce their employment capability, we had to complete a lot of paperwork to reflect the individual's limitations of employment. This would include many things such as could they be used as guards, working at heights, lifting, service overseas, in fact practically anything. There were different rules for aircrew and groundcrew, and it was an exact process. Compiling the limitations was one of the great mysteries of the trade, but once mastered was fairly straight forward. Unfortunately for Sergeant Fuller, he could not grasp the concept. Instead of saying to someone, "Look, would you show me how to do this." he always used the old trade training excuse. It took a while before I realised what he was up to and I have to confess that I had a little sympathy with him, as until you do finally understand the process, it is daunting. However, one day I had had enough of doing his work as well as my own. He gave me another medical board to do on an airman aircrew. As this was someone that the RAF had invested a great deal of money in through his training, the rules regarding aircrew are very strict and quite limiting. I completed the paperwork for the board and put it in an envelope. I then went into his office, with the medical documents of the individual to be boarded and told him that I found this one too difficult and could he show me what to do. He told me that he was a little busy and for me to just leave the file on his desk. I continued to press, saying that I wanted to learn what to do as I refused to let a bit of paperwork beat me. After a short argument, he realised I would not go away until he showed me what to do. He fudged his way through the paperwork and presented a solution that did not really fit the criteria. I then gave him the envelope with the solution in and told him that it was OK to ask junior members for advice. He never did though, and we continued to carry him.

On one occasion, there were two SAS soldiers coming to see one of the doctors for a medical examination prior to a flight in one of the Nimrods. Sergeant Fuller emptied the front office, telling us not to look through the windows at these 'secret soldiers'. When the doctor buzzed through asking for some forms to write down that (surprise, surprise) the soldiers were fit to go flying, he personally took the forms in but 'averted his eyes' by shielding them with his hand, blatantly turning his back probably believing that if he looked at the SAS soldiers he would be killed immediately. What a fine representative of the RAF. The doctor in this instance was a civilian called Heather Tobin who coincidentally, had a relative killed whilst serving with the SAS. I believe he was Trooper Tobin, the medical orderly killed during the Battle of Mirbat in 1972. For his actions he was awarded the posthumous Distinguished Conduct Medal. The battle itself became part of SAS Regimental history.

On one occasion, I was duty medic for the weekend and Doc Tobin was the duty doctor. I had decided to dispose of all the date expired drugs from the dispensary, by dissolving them in a bucket of boiling water and flushing the contents down the toilet. Doc Tobin was a great Doc and would remain in the medical centre for most of the weekend, watching all the old films that were on TV. We both sat in the crew-room watching a film, with me pouring more and more stuff into the bucket. It was quite warm in the building so there was a small fan moving the still air about. We became quite giggly and silly, but fortunately realised that something I had dissolved was making us light-headed. Several childish moments later, I poured the contents away and we spent the remainder of the day giggling about the whole incident. Good job that no one needed any emergency treatment!

I managed to get selected for two aeromed flights whilst I was at RAF Kinloss. The first was a man who was a chronic alcoholic. He needed to be transported to the RAF Hospital Wroughton in Swindon for detoxification. He was so bad that without a regular intake of alcohol, he would hallucinate and become quite violent. Doctor Tobin had the patient in a reasonably calm state when she decided that he really was an emergency admission. Unfortunately we were some six hundred odd miles from the hospital, and the RAF was always reluctant to admit their psychiatric patients to a civilian hospital. The only aircraft we could fly this chap in was a visiting senior officer's HS 125. These are really a large executive type jet that is used by senior officers as a taxi. The officer was not too pleased at having his personal transport commandeered but as it was declared a medical necessity, he had little choice. I was to have an overnight stay at the hospital, returning by way of a civilian flight with Dan Air from Gatwick to Inverness airport. Knowing that I would probably arrive at Wroughton late in the day, I decided to include a few cans of lager in my overnight bag.

The patient was settled and given some sedation before the flight and he seemed quiet prepared to make the trip. We strapped in the wide leather seats and readied ourselves for takeoff. The air steward made sure everything was in order and took his seat prior to takeoff. My patient lasted all of fifteen minutes before the telltale beads of sweat started to appear on his brow. He said that he was OK but I knew that I was in for an interesting trip. Five minutes later, he was beginning to get very fidgety and agitated. I asked the steward for a cup of something and he reluctantly brought some water. I tried several calming techniques with the patient but to no avail. He was now getting in a terrible state, trying to unbuckle his seatbelt saying he wanted to walk about. I told him that he couldn't, which didn't help him too much. In an act of sheer desperation, I got my overnight bag, pulled out a can of lager and gave it to him. If this didn't work I had no doubt that I would be fighting the man and trying to restrain him. I had never seen such a dependency on alcohol before although I had dealt with several alcoholics during my career. He practically tore the top off the can and greedily drank about half of the contents before taking the can from his mouth. The steward looked horrified and disappeared off in the direction of the cockpit. He came back a few minutes later and announced that it was against regulations to drink alcohol on a RAF aircraft. The instructions from the pilot were that I was to surrender the alcohol to the steward immediately. I told the steward that I would treat my patient any way I saw fit and if he would like to ask the pilot to come back and speak with me personally, I would explain all, as I did not want to speak through a middle man. The steward got the message and went away. Aircrew never knew what was wrong with the patients they flew, but I think everyone guessed what this chap was soon to be treated for. In no time at all, my patient had returned to a semi-calm state and appeared to be coping with the trip a little better. Just before we landed he again began his cold sweats and looked like he needed another beer. I told him to hang on until we had landed and I would give him another beer when we were in the car on the way to the RAF hospital at Wroughton. It must have been the longest twenty minutes of his life. I have never seen anyone get off a non-burning aircraft so quickly. Still, we were soon in the car and he was soon into his second can of lager - my lager! The remainder of the journey was quite uneventful and I soon handed over my patient to the duty nursing staff on the ward where the patient was to be admitted for detoxification. I found my accommodation and dutifully set off for the NAFFI to begin my own intoxication. Ironic really.

My second aeromed from Kinloss was far more interesting. I was lucky enough to be nominated to fly to Namibia and stay for a week before flying back with a patient who had sustained two broken legs in a road traffic accident. Easy job. My outward flight was very comfortable. I flew British Airways Business Class to Johannesburg and had a ten-hour delay before completing the final leg to Windhoek, capital city of Namibia. I had flown business class before and looked forward to the flight. All went very well until we started the descent into Johannesburg. I was sat on the row of seats next to one of the doors (loads of legroom), near to one of the toilet areas. A short while before we began the approach a passenger had gone into the toilet but had not come out again. I was finishing my in-flight breakfast so wasn't paying too much attention to what was going on. Shortly afterwards, the food trays were removed and the seatbelt and no smoking signs came on. Still no one exited from the toilet. The stewardess was walking up and down the aisle checking everyone had their seatbelts on and was where they should have been. Each time she passed the toilet she would politely knock on the door and tell the occupant to hurry up. After about half a dozen times, a male steward came to the toilet and shouted through the door. By now, I was giving this my full attention. The steward disappeared and returned almost immediately. He opened the toilet door from the outside and jumped back as a lifeless arm flopped onto the floor in front of him. Thinking that this was something out of the ordinary, I unbuckled my seatbelt and told the steward that I was a medic and could I be of any assistance. There was a short delay so I took it upon myself to extract the rather large male from the toilet floor and stretch him out on the floor in front of where I had been sitting a few seconds ago. The man's visible signs were not too good. He had blue lips and a glazed look in his eyes. His body was lifeless. A quick check confirmed that he was not breathing and did not have a pulse. It is true to say that the training just took over. Without thinking, I was into the full resuscitation protocol. Two breaths for every fifteen heart compressions. Occasional checking of vital signs. His colour improved slightly so I was confident that I was doing the right things. I wasn't confident that he would survive though. He looked too far gone. As I looked up during the pause between giving a breath of air, I caught sight of everyone in an aisle seat leaning into the aisle watching me. Quite a surreal experience. With all those witnesses I knew I would have to carry on giving resuscitation until we had landed and I estimated that to be about twenty to thirty minutes. It was going to be a long job.

I had been working on the man for about five minutes when the steward came back. I hadn't even noticed that he had gone somewhere. "Captain's complements," he said. "You'll have to return to your seat and fasten your seatbelt." I told him that as I had commenced resuscitation I had no intention of stopping. He persisted so I told him to get lost. In the end he stormed off again only to come back about a minute or two later. "The Captain said that if you don't sit down you will be arrested under aviation law and forcibly returned to your seat." he announced triumphantly. I glared at him and told him I was prepared to take the risk of not being strapped in on landing but he just repeated his previous comment. Jobsworth! Reluctantly, I rolled the man into the recovery position and returned to my seat some three feet away. To say I was angry was an understatement.

After what seemed the longest approach to an airport ever, the wheels of the aircraft finally touched the runway. As soon as the final wheel was on the ground, I unbuckled my belt and re-commenced resuscitation. One of the stewardesses then appeared carrying an ambu-bag. That is, in effect, a rubber mask with a big bag on the end. You put the mask over the casualty's face and squeeze the bag. This forces air into the casualty's lungs. I was furious. If they had produced this when I was told to sit down, I could have attempted to resuscitate the male from my seat. Anyway, I took the bag and carried on resuscitating until the aircraft came to a stop. The door eventually opened and a South African paramedic came on board. I shook my head as she approached and after listening to the man's chest with her stethoscope, confirmed that he was indeed deceased. We carried on working on him until he was off the aircraft and out of sight of the other passengers. The paramedic lifted his shirt and we saw a lengthy scar running the length of the chest. At some point he had had open-heart surgery. I hoped he had enjoyed his extra years. So much for this trip being an easy job. The cabin crew was really grateful for my help and gave me a large bottle of champagne from the first class section.

Namibia, formerly known as South West Africa, was a beautiful country from the air, and I looked forward to seeing it at close range. Getting into the country proved a little challenging though. I presented myself at immigration, passport in hand. A clerk, who asked me how long I would be staying in the country, took my passport off me. I replied that I didn't know as it all depended on whether my patient would be fit to travel. This caused a little problem. He told me that anyone entering the country had to have an exit date otherwise he would not allow entry. When I again explained that I was travelling under the authority of the British Government, he motioned for someone I presumed to be his senior officer. At no point did he offer my passport back. I got a little worried, but thought that there was little I could do at that precise moment in time. The senior officer arrived and asked me again how long I would be staying. I explained the purpose of my trip and said that someone from the British Embassy would be meeting me. I made no reference to being part of the military as I thought that would only cause more problems. He asked me where I would be staying and I replied that I wouldn't know until

I met my contact. More problems. This went on for about twenty minutes and I was convinced that I would be taken into an isolation room and given the third degree. In the end I said that I didn't care and that they could put me on the next flight back to Johannesburg. I would contact the British Embassy from there and all hell would probably break loose. I gave the attitude that I wasn't bothered but my mind was going like the clappers thinking of my next move. In the end the senior officer stamped my passport and said that I could stay for a period of no longer than one week. I said thank you, cleared immigration, collected my luggage and finally met my contact. So much for the easy job. My contact turned out to be an Army Staff Sergeant on detachment in the country. I had been given allowances, which were to be used for hotel bills etc, but I was invited to stay in the accommodation used by the Army guys. They were very good hosts and made me feel very welcome. I said that I would like to visit my patient in hospital so that I could do the introductions and ensure that he would be fit to fly in a week's time. Nothing was too much trouble for my host and we were soon driving along the dusty roads to the local hospital. On arrival, I was quite shocked by what I saw. The hospital was definitely third world. There were people in beds along the walls of the corridor and operations were being performed in side rooms with no doors to screen the process. Patients were wheeled into a room, operated on, and wheeled back out to the corridor. Fortunately for my patient, a Captain in the Army, the MoD had paid for a private room and was in the process of moving him to a private hospital later that day.

Introductions made, I explained the process of aeromedical evacuation to the Captain and asked how he had come to get both of his legs broken. He explained that he was part of a military team running in a sponsored event, raising money for local charities. As Namibia is such a hot country, it was decided that the run should take place early in the morning before the sun had risen too high, but with enough light for the runners to be seen. All precautions were taken with the runners being followed by a safety vehicle. The run had been going well until a driver had overtaken the safety vehicle at speed and swerved back in front of it, hitting the runner in front, which happened to be my patient. The motorist failed to stop initially, but was eventually stopped and detained. It turned out that he was the local doctor and had failed to stop because he was so drunk he shouldn't have been driving. By all accounts, the other runners gave the driver a good pasting before being handing him over to the police. The Captain was lucky to survive the incident. He suffered two broken legs and badly bruised internal organs. I kept my questions purely medical and limited to the quality of life issues for the wellbeing of my patient, and was glad I did. I had a slight inkling that all had not been revealed to me, when my suspicions were confirmed. An Army Major walked into the room in service uniform. In his pocket was a sand-coloured beret with a winged dagger cloth badge. These people were SAS. I was glad that I had not entered into the 'what are you doing here' routine as that gave me a little professional credibility. All initial checks completed I said farewell to my patient and wished him luck in his transfer to the private hospital the following morning.

My host then asked if I would like to go for a drive around to have a look at the area and I eagerly said yes. I was not disappointed. The country was just as beautiful on the ground as it was from the air. I couldn't believe that a short drive from the city took you out into the wide desert areas of Windhoek. On the way back into the city, I was asked if I would like to have a look at one of the 'shanty towns'. I said that I would and was advised that we would not be driving through too slowly and that I was to keep all windows up and the door locked. I slightly regretted saying that I would like to visit but felt that I could not miss the opportunity. It is difficult to put into words, but I was not prepared for the vision of extreme poverty on one side of the road and wealth on the other. Both communities existed within feet of each other. I wondered how this should be allowed to happen and even felt slightly embarrassed about being a white person. I have to say that it was a humbling moment.

Back at the accommodation there was little for me to do until the day before my patient and I were due to fly home. Unless, of course, he wanted me to do something for him. I took the opportunity to explore the city and thoroughly enjoyed my few days. I used the money I had to buy a week's worth of shopping for my hosts (there were three others in the house) as they had gone out of their way to make me feel welcome.

The day before the flight home, I re-visited the Captain, who was now in the private hospital. What a difference. It reminded me of the shanty town area, with this being the posh side of the road. Definitely a case of the haves and the have-nots. He was fit to fly so arrangements were made to have the stretchers fitted to the aircraft we would fly home on. Our trip took us from Windhoek to London with a ten-hour layover in Johannesburg.

Windhoek to Johannesburg was pleasant and uneventful and on arrival at Johannesburg I booked a room in the airport hotel so that the Captain could rest on a bed if he wanted to. I took the opportunity to rest, as I never slept during an aeromed flight. After a meal, we did the usual duty free trip prior to going through immigration. Fortunately, this time there were no problems and we were soon in the departure lounge. As we boarded the aircraft, I was surprised to see that it was the same crew that I had flown with to Johannesburg. One of the stewardesses who had helped in the resuscitation attempt recognised me and from then on, we wanted for nothing. The Captain was settled onto his stretcher, a purpose built bed which fitted over nine folded economy seats, and I sat across the aisle to him. A pre-flight drink of champagne was offered to us and we both took the glasses offered. I wouldn't drink when on duty so my patient ended up with two glasses. This was the home leg. The easy bit. After a few hours, I was pleased to see that the Captain had fallen asleep. This meant that either he was comfortable or that the champagne had taken effect. Either way I was pleased. I was watching the in-flight film when one of the stewardesses approached me and asked if I would take a look at another passenger. I agreed so long as someone kept an eye on my sleeping charge. I was taken to a Pakistani lady who was sitting in her seat in the economy section in front of the one where I was. She claimed to be suffering from asthma and said that the whole experience was claustrophobic for her. I didn't believe her and quietly told the stewardess that I thought she was trying to get herself upgraded to a better seat. I carried out a brief examination and could find nothing wrong. The Pakistani lady was hugging something in a plastic carrier bag and dramatically produced a battered old nebuliser claiming that she had to use it. Nebulisers are used by asthmatics to vaporise their medication for inhalation. By now she was beginning to make a bit of noise and started to disturb other passengers. I asked if I could try to get the nebuliser working by plugging it into a shaver socket in one of the toilets. The captain of the aircraft agreed and an unsuccessful attempt made. The woman was still creating a scene. In desperation, I asked the stewardess for a jug of boiling water. She looked puzzled but nevertheless went off to get one. When she returned I poured the water into the bowl of the nebuliser and then added one of the ampoules of her medication to the water. I then pushed her head over the bowl and told her to breathe deeply. Realising that there was no upgrade forthcoming, she leant forward breathing in the steam from the bowl. That is how I left her as I walked back to my seat. My patient had missed all the excitement as he was still sleeping soundly. Easy job. Fortunately nothing else happened on the flight and I handed over the patient to nursing staff from Woolwich Hospital on our arrival in

London. On a later trip to Hereford, I saw a beautiful picture of an African sunrise on the wall of the Sergeants and Warrant Officers' Mess. The memories of my trip to Namibia came back to me. On closer inspection of the picture, I saw that it had been presented to them by my former patient!

Not very much else out of the ordinary happened whilst I was at RAF Kinloss. The station Padre, Squadron Leader Garry Burton, became a good friend of the family and we got into trouble after he and I ended up quite drunk at the Medical Centre Christmas party one year. Fortunately, I blamed him, and he blamed me, and since the culprit couldn't be identified, we somehow managed to get away with it – although we both had huge hangovers! He was also a great help to everyone after the sudden and unexpected death of my dad.

Several months later, dad must have been looking down on me as there was a knock on the door and Sergeant Fuller was there. He said he was the bringer of good news but I had to answer "Yes" to the first question he asked. I knew he was an idiot so refused and told him to just tell me the news. He said that I had been successful on the recent promotion board and would be promoted to sergeant myself, on completion of a few courses. I asked where I was going to be posted, remembering the man with the sense of humour deep in the postings cell of Command. After what seemed an eternity he told me that I was going to RAF Odiham. RAF Odiham – home of the Puma and Chinook helicopter squadrons. I was being promoted and posted to the very station I wanted to go to.

Thank you dad. Up yours sense of humour man! I was so happy. In a few months time I was to leave RAF Kinloss and North Scotland. If I was honest, there were few happy memories although I would miss some of the personalities. I counted Doctor Tobin and the padre Garry Burton amongst the few that I would miss. However, if I never saw my sergeant again, it would be too soon. He had been quite a challenge!

Although it had only been eighteen months since we had arrived from Hong Kong, we were all pleased to be going back to England. We had no ill feeling towards Scotland; it was just that we felt so far away from our families. We had been quite depressed when we had packed up in Hong Kong, but this time we were almost singing as we packed. Eventually, our world was back in cardboard boxes and we headed off for RAF Odiham in Hampshire. Little did I know what was in store for me there!

Training in the desert prior to the Gulf War. A few days later all our helicopters would be covered in random black paint markings, as this current paint scheme was too bright for night operations.

LSVs. Toys for the boys.

With the mountains of Oman visible in the distance, this was home for three days. My 'tent' is in the bottom right of the picture.

The picture of Pauline and Mark that was with me throughout the Gulf War. I had it pinned inside my mosquito net!

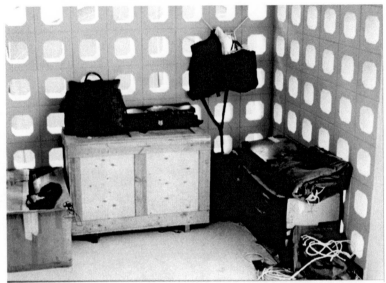

The medical area at Al Jewf. The hand made light proof casualty tent can be seen on the cardboard box on the right of the picture.

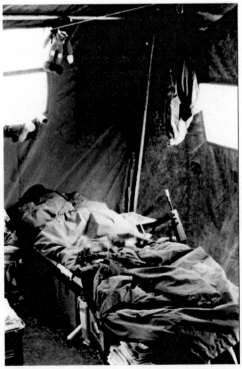

My bed space in the tent at Al Jewf. The arctic parka over the sleeping bag was to keep me warm during the freezing nights.

PROMISORY NOTE

HM BRITANNIC GOVERNMENT PROMISES TO PAY THE BEARER OF THIS NOTE THE SUM OF £5000 STERLING PROVIDING YOU DO NOT HARM THE PERSON ISSUING IT AND THAT YOU ASSIST HIM TO EITHER EVADE CAPTURE OR RETURN HIM TO EITHER SAUDI ARABIA OR TO NEUTRAL TERRITORY. TO CLAIM THE REWARD YOU SHOULD TAKE THIS NOTE TO ANY BRITISH EMBASSY OR CONSULATE AND ASK TO SPEAK TO THE DEFENCE ATTACHE OR ONE OF HIS ASSISTANTS. HE WILL THEN GIVE YOU THE SUM OF £5000.

سند اذني

تتعهد الحكومة البريطانية بالدفع لحامل هذا السند الاذني مبلغ ٥٠٠٠ جنيه استرليني شرطاً الا تضر الفرد المصدر له و شرطاً ان تساعده في تفادي الاسر او ان تقوم باعادته الى المملكة العربية السعودية او الى ارض محايدة . من اجل اخذ المكافأة عليك تقديم هذا السند الى سفارة او قنصلية بريطانية وطلب الالتقاء بالملحق الدفاعي او احد معاونيه . ثم سوف يعطي لك المبلغ المحدد اي ٥٠٠٠ جنيه استرليني .

سند اذني

تتعهد الحكومة البريطانية بالدفع لحامل هذا السند الاذني مبلغ ٥٠٠٠ جنيه استرليني شرطاً الا تضر الفرد المصدر له وشرطاً ان تساعده في تفادي الاسر او ان تقوم باعادته الى المملكة العربية السعودية او الى ارض محايدة . من اجل اخذ المكافأة عليك تقديم هذا السند الى سفارة او قنصلية بريطانية وطلب الالتقاء بالملحق الدفاعي او احد معاونيه . ثم سوف يعطي لك المبلغ المحدد اي ٥٠٠٠ جنيه استرليني .

My 'Goolie Chit'. Issued to me in case I needed to escape from behind enemy lines. Fortunately, there was never a need to cash it in.

151

The border of Saudi Arabia and Iraq, waiting for the SAS to return
after five weeks behind enemy lines.

One of several SAS 'Pinkies' to return safely. In all there were
about twenty vehicles in the column.

Leaving RAF Odiham to take part in the Gulf War Victory Flypast over London. Ramp Riding really was an excellent way to travel!

Most tasks were either early morning or during the night. This was taken early morning somewhere in the South of France.

The building with the damaged shutter was our accommodation during a week long stay in the South of France. Not all accommodation was as nice as this.

One of the better rooms was used as the medical centre!

Helicasting.
It is, without doubt, one of the best ways I have ever gone to work.

Chapter 8

Pauline and Mark stayed in Scotland for a few weeks until a married quarter became available. While waiting for a quarter, I was to live in the Senior NCO's Mess. It was quite daunting, driving through the main gate of RAF Odiham for the first time. The difference between junior ranks and senior ranks is quite marked in the RAF. It was something I had to get used to. That said, I didn't really think much of rank. I would, of course, respect the rank of the individual, but I used to work on the theory that I had the rank of medic and everybody else had the rank of patient. After all, a Group Captain's hemorrhoids were just as painful as an airman's! They all needed the same care and treatment.

Arriving at the Medical Centre I was pleased to see that the Flight Sergeant was Terry Hampton. The last time I had seen Terry was when I was going through training and he was a Corporal instructor, teaching the course ahead of mine. He had taken me for a few subjects and was not only a good instructor, but a very likeable person too. He appeared genuinely pleased to see me when I arrived at his office. Holding out his hand in welcome he congratulated me on my promotion and in the next breath said, "It's my job to prepare you for promotion to Flight Sergeant." Talk about knowing how to motivate people! We spent the next hour or so talking about my role in the medical centre and the fact that I would be attached to one of the helicopter squadrons as their medic. The main role of the sergeant medics at RAF Odiham was to be available to move with one of the helicopter squadrons whenever they went on deployment, or were tasked away from the main camp for any length of time. The sergeant medic was to provide the medical support to everyone whilst away from the camp. When not on deployment or task, they would look after the running of either the main admin office or the medical stores. Terry Hampton asked if I would mind looking after the medical stores side of things. I made out that I didn't mind, but was really very pleased. I wasn't one for doing a lot of paperwork! The other medical sergeant at Odiham was Danny Gibson. He would become my mentor for the next few months until I found my feet. Danny was attached to 33 Squadron and did not wish to change, so I was to become the medic to 7 Squadron. 33 Squadron was a Puma helicopter squadron whilst 7 Squadron was a Chinook helicopter squadron.

Number 7 Squadron was formed on 1 May 1914 at Farnborough in Hampshire. Although the Squadron broke up after three months, it reformed in the September and was sent to France to carry out bomber and reconnaissance missions. The Squadron completed many missions before being disbanded in 1919. One of the missions during the First World War resulted in Captain J A Liddell being awarded a posthumous Victoria Cross. The Squadron was brought together again as a bomber unit, in 1923. In the early part of the Second World War, the Squadron was equipped with the Shorts Stirling bomber aircraft, however in 1943 they joined the Pathfinder Force and took delivery of the Avro Lancaster, flying mainly night bomber missions for the remainder of the war. During the war years the Squadron flew 5060 missions, lost 157 aircraft and 800 aircrew. 546 aircrew were to receive medals and honours. The Squadron was again disbanded on 1 January 1956 but some eleven months later on 1 November, the Squadron reformed and took delivery of the Valiant aircraft. Retaining the role of a bomber squadron, 7 Squadron would form part of the V-Force. This lasted for two years before being disbanded yet again. In May 1970, 7 Squadron reformed, this time with the Canberra aircraft. Their role this time was as a target facility squadron. Twelve years later the Squadron changed to its current role of a Chinook Helicopter Squadron, and changed its base to that of RAF Odiham in Hampshire. This has been their home ever since.

I really didn't mind which squadron I was to work on, as I was back in the helicopter world. Being a Squadron medic meant having responsibility to the Squadron personnel when away from the main station. There were two doctors at RAF Odiham with one 'attached' to each Squadron. However, they never left the unit to go on deployment with their Squadron, and the medical cover was provided by Danny Gibson or myself, depending on which Squadron was away.

While I was living in the mess there was little to do in the evenings so I set about learning the Chinook airframe in detail as I wanted to become as involved as possible. I chuckled to myself as I remembered the episode of me falling through the floor in the Falkland Islands. I memorized all of the escape routes, where all power points and fire extinguishers were stowed and other emergency items such as first aid kits, asbestos gloves and fire axe. It was the closest I was going to get to regular flying so I wanted to make a good impression. Over the next few days I made my introductions to all on the Squadron and, for a non-regular squadron person, I was well accepted. I was told that my first deployment with the Squadron would be on what was called Operation Sanctuary. This was a once a year deployment used primarily to accustom the new personnel to life in the field. The deployment was scheduled for September time and was well timed as Pauline and Mark were due to move down from Scotland in July, as a married quarter had finally become available. At least they would have time to settle before I started what would be regular absences from home.

Our married quarter was at a small village called Church Crookham, about eight miles from Odiham. It was really good to be living back as a family, and I was really settled. Across the road from where we lived was a large garden centre, which we visited on a regular basis. As we lived a distance from the main camp, it was like being a 'civvi' who just happened to work on a RAF station. I couldn't have been happier. Pauline also went back to nursing, and was really doing well at Frimley Park Hospital.

Packing for my first field deployment was what could loosely be described as a nightmare. I had never been on a field deployment before and did not know what to expect. The exercise lasted a week but I must have packed enough kit to last for a year! I had enough medical kit to probably treat everyone on the exercise if they all went sick at the same time - and still have some kit left over! Still, it was a learning process for me. Once my kit had been packed it had to be taken to the Squadron so that it could be loaded onto a helicopter. I drew one or two glances as I unloaded my five metal lacon containers from the back of the ambulance and placed them on the hangar floor. One of the helicopter loadmasters came up to me and said that my predecessor only used to take a maximum of two and had I packed the entire medical centre. I reassured him that I had only packed what I thought necessary and walked off trying to give of an air of confidence whilst all the time doubting if I had got any of it right. No doubt there were several comments made as I drove away in the ambulance.

The next morning I arrived at the Squadron hangar and helped load all the equipment that was going with us on board the helicopters. Once everything was ready, the ground crew took up what little space was left. We would climb over the equipment, neatly stacked along the centre of the cabin floor and squeeze ourselves into the seats along the cabin sides. Once everyone was on board and seated, the aircraft auxiliary power units began their high pitch whine as the engines were started and the cabin gently rocked as the twin rotors began to turn. The smell of aviation fuel was overpowering. All preliminary checks completed by the crew, the Chinook began moving slowly along the taxiway before lining up on the runway ready for clearance to take off. The noise from the rotors changed and we lifted smoothly into the air. After take off checks completed, the two loadmasters took up their positions at either end of the cabin and began their navigation and observation tasks. I would soon realise that it took four people to fly a Chinook. Two pilots at the front and two crewmen in the back. It really was a team effort. Obviously, the pilots were responsible for flying the aircraft, one being the handling pilot (actually hands on the flying controls) whilst the other pilot, known as the non-handling pilot would monitor such matters as the navigation, radio transmissions and engine temperatures and pressures. The two crewmen would monitor navigation, assist in radio transmissions and also monitor all things engines amongst other things.

During the flight I was constantly thinking what was expected from me during the next week, and reassuring myself that I could cope with whatever was to come my way. After about an hour or so, we landed alongside a wooded area next to a disused railway siding somewhere in central England. This was to be our forward operating base and home for the next week. Almost immediately after the rotors had stopped turning, people sprang into action. Kit was being unloaded and different sections were being set up. Catering would go in one of the brick structures, as there was still a water outlet. I would go in the opposite corner of the building and the engineering equipment would go in the other brick structure. All accommodation would be in tents in the wooded area. The toilets were sited a little distance away from the living area and well away from the catering section. The toilets were in fact dustbins lined with heavy duty dustbin liners, into which was poured a measure of chemical, designed to combat bacteria and odour. The toilets were sited in an old brick structure that had no roof or door. Improvisation was the deployed airman's best friend and the toilet area soon had a door made from hanging a hessian sheet and a roof of corrugated iron sheeting. Everyone's equipment and kit was just left in the area where they would be using it and it was up to the individual to set everything up. This included your tent. Some smart Alec said that I had only brought so many lacons so that I could build myself somewhere to live rather than put a tent up. I have to say that it didn't take too long to get everything set up and get into the swing of things. The first day passed quickly and we were all told to get a good night's sleep, as the exercise would start in earnest the following morning.

We woke bright and early to torrents of rain. The ground looked like something out of the Somme. It was going to be a long week. After a good breakfast we had our first briefing. We were told about three different factions fighting over some made up country and that we were there as a peacekeeping force. After the briefing we all agreed that it sounded rather similar to the current problems in the Balkans. My day usually started with a small sick parade where those who felt particularly ill could come and see me for diagnosis and treatment. There were always one or two first thing, but everyone knew that they could come and see me anytime. I was an unknown quantity at first and I think one or two came to see me just to find out what I was like. People expecting to get the day off for something trivial were usually disappointed. During the week, my confidence increased and I found that I was actually enjoying myself. There was little for me to do medically and I made sure that I found other work to keep me occupied and to free up the engineers so that they could get on with what they did best. I always made sure that I toured the entire site on a daily basis.

Presumably because I had worked so much with the Army, I had forged a particularly good relationship with the Squadron Regiment section. The Regiment guys were the RAF equivalent of the Army and their primary task was that of airfield or location security. In other words, during times of conflict, shoot anyone trying to gain unauthorized access to the military base! They used to take the mickey out of me accusing me of being 'just a medic'. It was all done in good fun with everyone soon realizing that I really didn't care about rank, or trade, at all. The Chinooks were flying in and out of the site on a regular basis, carrying out different taskings. Standing around one time, a group of us watched one of the Chinooks fly back towards the landing area. Instead of going to land, it hover taxied towards the toilet area. A hover taxi is where the helicopter maintains its height whilst moving slowly in whatever direction the pilot chooses. The downwash from a Chinook is fierce at the best of times, and when it is hovering about twenty feet off the ground it is quite severe. As the Chinook approached the toilets, the corrugated tin roof began to rattle about. The Chinook crept a little nearer. The roof rattled a bit more and started to flap up and down. The Chinook crept a little nearer. The roof flapped a little more before lifting off completely, turning side on and dropping like a guillotine blade. The next thing we saw was one of the chief engineers stomping off to the landing area where the Chinook had quickly retreated. The engineer had not even pulled his trousers up as he approached the Chinook, still with its rotors turning. He banged on the side window where the pilot was sitting and must have been screaming and shouting at him. His arms were waving about but all we could hear was the noise of the rotor blades. The pilot was in hysterics, as were the crewmen looking out through the door and the rest of us lucky enough to have seen the whole thing. Realizing he would get nowhere, the engineer stormed back to the toilet, threw the roof out and presumably carried on where he left off prior to his little meeting with the pilot.

I suppose it could have been quite a serious accident if the roof had landed on his head. Fortunately it didn't.

It continued to rain throughout the week and the fields just got muddier and muddier. Morale remained high thanks to little incidents such as the one recounted above.

Towards the end of the week, we had to defend our camp from supposed intruders. This was the ground defence training part of the week. Our attackers were going to be the RAF Regiment guys. They had threatened to capture me and beat me half to death, so I had accepted the challenge telling them that they had all better come together as opposed to individually. I had been issued with a sub-machine gun (SMG) for use only in protection of my patients or myself. It was against the Geneva Convention for me to carry arms for any other reason. The RAF being as efficient as ever had no blank ammunition for the SMGs so those of us issued with one had to walk around with a useless weapon and two empty magazines. I had locked my SMG in one of the lacons for most of the week, until someone noticed that I wasn't carrying it everywhere. I was duly chastised, and carried my dead weight everywhere with me after that. During the defence phase, my day changed little. I was still the only medic so stayed close to my kit waiting for the 'injured' to be brought to me. All engineers not on aircraft duty were deployed around the camp perimeter on guard duty, to ensure that no intruders could get in and cause us trouble. There was no one about for me to talk to so I began to wander around the small building that housed the medical area. Looking through one of the holes in the brick wall alongside my kit I saw one of the Regiment guys sneaking through the woods towards the camp. He was intent on getting into the camp to create mayhem, so had not noticed that I had seen him. I waited patiently for him to get closer not daring to move in case my movement attracted his attention. He got to within about twenty feet of where I was standing and I thought it about the right time to spoil his day. Unfortunately, I didn't have any ammunition so just pointed my empty SMG at him and said, "Click, your dead." He turned to see my smiling face and said, "Bugger off Bri, I'm busy." before just walking off! I was most disappointed but at least if he got into the camp, I would have something to do. Shortly afterwards, all hell broke loose, with gunfire going off all over the place. Our 'war' raged for a few hours before the alarm call went out requiring all of us to wear our nuclear, biological and chemical (NBC) protective suit. We then knew that the war would be over in a few more hours, as that was how all our wars went. Not only that, but we were due to return to RAF Odiham the following day! One of the Regiment guys was brought to me as a 'casualty' so I set about treating him. I had my SMG on a sling about my shoulder so pushed the weapon behind my back. As I bent over to examine my casualty, the weapon shot around to the front and hit the Regiment guy square on the forehead. He looked a little stunned, declared himself fully cured and stood up refusing all treatment. Everyone who saw it was crying with laughter and eventually the guy who was hit was laughing too. It was a pure accident but because he had been one of the Regiment guys threatening to do me in, I told everybody that it was because of the threats that I had hit him. It started a great rivalry between the Regiment guys and me that lasted the whole of my time with the Squadron. Not long after my unprovoked assault, it was decided that we had won the war and, after another good meal, everyone started to pack equipment away ready for the return flight back to Odiham the following morning. I had survived my first deployment.

Back at camp the following day, I re-packed my kit so that it would be ready for the next time. I think it took me about half an hour at the most.

In between deployments I made the most of my time in the stores area of the medical centre. Danny Gibson looked after the office side of things whilst I looked after the stores. Wherever possible, I used to make arrangements to visit the Squadron to carry out 'checks' on kit and anything else that I could convince people needed checking. I also used the time to get in as much flying as possible. All the crewmen were senior NCO ranks and I got on with the majority of them really well. I think it amused them that a medic wanted to fly so often but I really was like a dog with two tails. I couldn't get enough flying! Many a time the crew would try to either get me to throw up or to try to scare me. Thankfully they failed on all but one occasion when I managed to hide the fact that I seriously considered being frightened.   On that particular flight I was ramp riding. That is sitting on the rear of the ramp with my legs dangling in the breeze as the helicopter flew along and doing nothing but admire the view. It was a fantastic way to fly and perfectly safe as I was wearing a safety harness that was secured around my waist at one end and to the floor at the other end. Immersed in my own little world, I was tapped on the shoulder by one of the crewmen. As I turned around to see what he wanted, his big smiley face lunged towards me obscuring my view of everything else. As the horrendous image backed away I could see that he was holding the floor end of my harness in his hand. The other crewman was laughing his head off and I could hear the pilots laughing over the radio. At that moment the pilots began to, how can I put this, not exactly fly straight and level. I am sure that my eyes went as big as dinner plates and I am convinced that my backside took on the suction power of a limpet. I was convinced that I was going to fall out of the back of the helicopter. However, I don't know how I managed but I think I gave the appearance of remaining relatively calm under the circumstances and just shrugged before turning back around and looking out of the back again. I thought, if I'm going to die at least they could say I did it with style. I was then handed the other end of the harness, given a pat on the shoulder and left to my own devices. I waited for as long as I dared before turning around to 'casually' secure my harness to the floor again. As I did, I noticed a second harness leading from another floor ring to the back of my harness.   The loadmaster had attached it without my knowledge and I had been in no danger whatsoever. I saw that particular trick performed many times after that and laughed just as much as everyone else.

When not on deployment, I took on the responsibility of running the medical stores and dispensary. Working in that department with me, were a corporal and a senior aircraftsman. They would run the department during my many absences. I have to say that I preferred working in the stores as opposed to working in the admin office. I never was one for routine paperwork. Stores also gave you the additional challenge of ensuring that there was always enough stock of medicines for the doctors to prescribe. Occasionally we got it wrong and had to ask the doctors to prescribe something else. Occasionally, our suppliers, the Defence Medical Equipment Depot (DMED), failed to deliver items within the specified times, but on the whole we managed to get the job done. Every now and again, the medical supplier used to change the ordering procedure without bothering to tell anyone. We used to order needles for syringes in boxes of 100. An order had been submitted for three units (i.e. 300 needles). The supplier had changed the ordering to individual items, so very kindly sent us three needles in an envelope and expected us to make them last for five months. One telephone call later saw three boxes of 100 needles put in the post for us. I did hear a story of someone ordering something in the region of 5000 paracetamol tablets (the unit of order being one tablet) and receiving 5000 bottles of 100. Telephone calls to his friends in and around the area soon disposed of the excess.

I was thoroughly enjoying myself at RAF Odiham. Pauline had returned to nursing and Mark had settled in school. I decided that I was going to achieve a life-long ambition and pass my motorcycle test. I bought a Honda CG125 and after taking and passing the Compulsory Basic Test in a football club car park, took to the roads on two wheels. Great fun. It wasn't long before I applied for my full test. I knew that the test would be held in and around the Aldershot area so began riding there at every opportunity. I wanted to know the road layout so that there would be no suprises around any corners on the test. When the test day arrived, I was pleased to find out that I had covered the majority of the route during my many practice runs. The examiner was very pleasant and passed me first time despite the fact that, when we returned to the test centre, with the examiner following me in his car, I turned into the car park through the exit only route. He put it down to nerves, but if the truth be known, hadn't seen the sign. I left the centre with pass certificate firmly secured in my jacket pocket and a big grin on my face.

In August 1991, the news was full of reports that Saddam Hussain had invaded the country of Kuwait. Wherever you went, information was on the TV or radio. It was also the talk of the camp. Rumor on the Squadron was that we would be out there soon. At that time, I chose not to tell Pauline, as there was no certainty that anyone would be going anywhere. The mood on the Squadron, however, changed dramatically. Everyone was more serious. The training became more geared towards a desert environment and, for the first time in many years, I actually listened during the training and lectures of chemical and biological warfare. This was serious stuff. I read as much as I could about medical issues concerning life in a desert region and also the medical books on chemical and biological issues. If I was off somewhere unpleasant, I wanted to be able to do my job well. I was also under the impression that if we did deploy to something as big and potentially dangerous as this we would be taking one of the doctors with us. I later found out that would not be the case. I would be the primary RAF medical specialist for the whole deployment.

Saddam Hussain's reputation went before him. Most of us had heard that he had already used chemical weapons against his own people. There was a belief that he would not hesitate to use them on anyone else, especially western infidels. With the Falkland Islands, there had been an initial 'where are they then?' pause before the military machine swung into action. There was also little thought towards unconventional warfare. The invasion of Kuwait, however, was a totally different matter. We all knew it was in the Middle East and that there was a madman, with access to weapons of mass destruction, behind it. On the Squadron, preparations continued. Aircraft were made ready and additional safety features added, such as chaff and flare dispensers and infra-red protection. I was building up my medical equipment, constantly adding and removing items. Right up until the last minute I was not sure that I had packed the right items or even whether I had packed enough. Time would tell. It was also confirmed that there would be no doctor going with me. I would be on my own providing primary medical care. To say I felt a little worried would be an understatement. That said, I was confident in my own abilities as a medic.

During late September and October I had been preparing both Pauline and myself for the fact that I might be going off to war. Things on occasion became tense although we never let anything get too far. We were both nervous. Mark was only four years old, so did not really understand what was going on. He had become used to me going away from home for periods so thought nothing unusual was going on. Pauline and I encouraged him to think that way.

Late in October 1990, I attended a Squadron briefing by the Wing Commander. Everyone who was to be sent to the Middle East was called together. We arrived in the briefing room and sat around nervously. All went quiet as the Wing Commander walked in. "Gentlemen," he started, You will deploy overseas on November 24th. As you are the Special Forces Flight, you will be told your destination when you are at the airport. I advise you to make preparations regarding provisions for your families. I don't know how long you will be away at this time. Any questions?" There was stunned silence. The Wing Commander seized the opportunity of silence and disappeared out of the room. My brain was working overtime. "Special Forces Flight.......November 24th.....provisions...........don't know how long......
I had heard of the Special Forces Flight and knew some of the crew. I never thought I would go to war with them. There was so little said by the Wing Commander, but there were massive implications. How was I going to tell Pauline? "I'm off to war now dear. I don't know where I'm going or how long I'll be away, but don't worry." That was a difficult time for everyone. We had, of course been sworn to secrecy so, at work, only the Flight Sergeant and

Senior Medical Officer knew my departure date up until about a week or so before we left. I had packed and re-packed both my medical and personal kit so many times I could probably have done it in my sleep.

Several of us took the opportunity to contact our insurance companies with a view to increasing our life assurance. Everyone knew that the planned operation was going to be called Operation Granby, but our little trip was called something else. It was quite satisfying answering the insurance agent's question about whether or not I was going on Operation Granby. "I can honestly tell you that I'm not going on Granby." I managed to say with a straight face. Now, had he asked me whether I was going to the Gulf, I might have been worried about handing him my completed life assurance form. Ah well, the quality of the question always reflects the answer. I had the satisfaction of knowing that if it all went wrong, Pauline and Mark would be well provided for.

The dreaded day arrived and I piled my kit into the boot of the car. Pauline was going to stay with her sister in Felixtowe so I decided not to prolong the agony by sitting at home all day waiting to drive to camp. Even though we weren't due to leave RAF Odiham until 4.00pm in the afternoon, I had decided that I would wait in the Medical Centre from mid-morning, giving Pauline enough time to reach her sisters before it went dark. I was pleased that Pauline and Mark were going to stay with family, as in times of crisis a family is the best thing going. I drove from our house to the camp and pulled up outside of the Medical Centre. I didn't want to hang about too long, as the parting process was painful enough as it was. I had been on several deployments since arriving at Odiham. Although I enjoyed the job I was doing, I always hated the initial leaving home bit. However, this was totally different. It is really difficult to describe the feeling of leaving your family knowing that you are off to what is probably going to be war. No matter what I did, I couldn't get the thought 'I wonder if this will be the last time I...' out of my head. I didn't say anything though. I kissed Mark and Pauline. Told them both I loved them, picked up my bags and disappeared into the Medical Centre without a backward glance. I walked straight into my office and just sat there. I was so close to breaking down in tears. I heard the car pull away and, after a short while, Alex Owens, the weekend duty medic, walked into my office and simply put a mug of tea in front of me, patted me on the shoulder and walked out. He knew there was nothing to say so he simply didn't. I was so grateful for that simple action. I had felt so alone up until that point. Eventually, I drank my tea, composed myself and went up to the crew room to talk to Alex. There were only a few hours left before I would leave for war.

Chapter 9

The walk to the Squadron seemed to take much longer than usual. I was loaded down with my kitbag and rucksack. On arrival at the Squadron, I dumped my kit and headed off for a cup of tea in the crewroom. There were others milling around but no one was in a mood for chatting. Eventually, we were called outside and started to load our kit on the coach that had arrived. Once on board, the driver was ordered off the coach and the door shut behind him by the Wing Commander. All went quiet. "Gentleman," he said, "Your destination is Abu Dhabi in the United Arab Emirates. You are the advance party for the Special Forces element of the war, should it come to that. Good luck and do the job that you have trained for." With that, he opened the door and was gone. The driver got back on and we were off. Some family members had come to see their loved ones off, but I was glad that Pauline was not there. I felt miserable. I gave the impression that I was reading a book but someone looking closely would have noticed that I was not turning any of the pages.

Initially, we drove in silence but it wasn't long before the military humour in adversity started. By the time we arrived at RAF Mildenhall, the American Air Force base we were flying out from, everyone was in a buoyant mood. I nearly had my first casualty before we had even left the country. One of the engineers had walked straight into a glass door, hitting it so hard he almost knocked himself out. There was a beautiful face print left on the glass though! Before too long we were loaded onto the massive C5 Galaxy transport aeroplane that would fly us to our first destination in the Middle East. On board were two of the Chinook helicopters that would be used by the Flight. Prior to take off we were given the usual pre-flight briefing by the loadmaster. It was one of the funniest things I had heard. He advised us that if there was an emergency we would all die, as he couldn't be bothered to tell us about the many escape routes, claiming the flight would be over by the time he finished. He also said that the chances were we wouldn't survive the crash anyway so there wasn't much point in giving us the briefing. When telling us how to don the life preservers he reminded us about the position used when "throwing up in the john after too much Budweiser". "You put your head through the hole the same as you put your head in the toilet." He simply said. The guy was fantastic. He knew that everyone was a little tense and did a great job in relaxing us.

The flight to the Middle East was uneventful and, after a short stop-over at an American Air Force base in Spain, we landed at a United Arab Emirates airfield and began to unload all our equipment. It did not take too long to carry all the kit into the secure hangar and get the two helicopters off the Galaxy. Once everything had been completed, we were told to get changed out of our military clothing into some civilian clothes. After a few of us exchanged puzzled looks we were told that for the first few weeks we would be staying in a local hotel. Things just got better! Once everyone was ready we were taken to the Intercontinental Hotel in Abu Dhabi. It was, like all hotels in the region, a luxury hotel. We had been told to leave all our military kit behind at the air-head so some blokes had had to unpack their clothes from military kit bags and carry their stuff in plastic bags. Here was the elite of the RAF helicopter world booking into a luxury hotel, carrying their belongings in carrier bags! The hotel staff were unaware of who we were but it must have looked like a coach full of bagmen arriving. I was to share a room with the operations guy, Stan Young. He was smaller than I was so I christened him 'Stumpy'. Unfortunately, a name that he was stuck with from then on. He was, and still is, a great bloke.

The following day we returned to the airfield that we had landed at the night before. It was a place called Bateen. The helicopters had been placed outside of two hardened shelters ready to be taken inside for the engineers to work on. However, in the light of the morning it became apparent that the aircraft would not fit inside the hangars and the engineers would be working outside most of the time. I began to set up the medical centre area. It would be in half of a portacabin with the other half being used by the safety equipment guys. Fortunately, there was very little for me to do medically. Apart from the odd minor complaint I kept myself busy by taking on several other jobs such as postman and odd-job man. I had liased with my Arabic medical counterparts on the camp and also with the small American contingent on the other side of the airfield. One morning, I was sat reading when someone rushed into the medical centre and shouted that someone had been hit in the face with a torque wrench. I grabbed my medical bergen and rushed out to the waiting car. As we were zooming towards the accident I was told that the engineer was working in the confined space of the rear pylon of the Chinook. He was tightening something up with the torque wrench which, due to the sweat on his hands, suddenly slipped from his grip. The wrench had shot back and hit him in the face. As I got out of the car I was expecting the worst, but all I saw as the engineer sitting on the floor next to the Chinook. No blood anywhere but he looked quite pale. Apparently, as the wrench was hurtling back at him he began to scream "Oh ****". Whilst shouting the "Oh" bit, the wrench hit him in the mouth at the point his mouth was wide open. There was no damage other than a small chip to one tooth. Lucky bloke. After a while, when he had settled down, I gave him my diagnosis that he escaped with minor damage because he had a big mouth. Other than that incident, there was little to test my medical skills. There had been an occasion where a Chinook crewman needed dental care due to raging toothache. I was a medic, not a dentist. I had some emergency dental cavity paste, which I offered him, but he refused, insisting on seeing a dentist. I arranged for him to see a dentist attached to the hotel and his problem was, thankfully, treated.

My main responsibility was to ensure that all the engineers were drinking enough water, as all their work was outdoors. As we were now becoming a secluded unit, I was getting a little worried about whether I would be able to cope on my own, should this escalate into a full blown war situation. I didn't let my feelings be known though. I reassured myself that others would be feeling the same. I was, however, constantly reading my medical books and quietly running through different scenarios with imaginary casualties.

A couple of weeks later, the main body of SAS arrived. A few of us went to the air-head at Bateen to help them unload some of their equipment. One of the C5 Galaxy aircraft taxied to a halt, and we watched as the front of the massive aircraft lifted up so as to allow access to the hold area. I was walking towards it with a Warrant Officer from the SAS when we saw the Galaxy aircrew jump off the front of the loading bay and sprint off towards one of the airport buildings. The Warrant looked at me and asked what they were doing. I said it was aircrew mentality and that it would be something like 'last one to the wall buys the ice-creams'. We arrived at the Galaxy and looked into the hold. It was completely full. On the right hand side were rows of Light Support Vehicles, known as LSVs or desert buggies. On the left hand side stretching from the front to the back and from the floor to the ceiling of the hold were boxes and boxes of all things explosive. There were rounds of ammunition, plastic explosive, grenades, missiles and goodness knows what else. It was then we noticed the black smoke coming from the back of the hold. There was a fire on the aircraft. So that's why the aircrew had run away! I looked at the SAS guy and said, "Last one to the wall buys the ice-creams?" "No point," he replied, "If that lot goes up it'll take everything out for miles. We might as well wait here and see what happens." Not wishing to be a chicken in front of him, I agreed, trying to sound as confident as I could. I just hoped that being vaporised would not be too painful. Before too long the fire service arrived and extinguished the small electrical fire. My reputation of being a bit of a nutter on the Squadron had received a substantial boost.

With all kit and personnel safely deployed to the region, training began in earnest. It had been decided that I might be needed to fly on missions, be they insertion or extraction missions, just in case my medical skills might be required. I therefore thought a little desert survival training might come in handy. I hoped never to have to use any newly acquired survival skills but thought it prudent to have at least a little knowledge. Just prior to moving out of Bateen for our next location, three others and I were dropped off in the desert, miles from anywhere and with only a small segment of a parachute and some bottles of water. "See you in three days time." Was the last thing I heard as I left the back of the Chinook. Over in the distance was the border with the Oman; a place that features prominently in the history of the SAS Regiment. Our survival instructor was one of the helicopter crewmen by the name of Wes Hogan. He was a good friend and went to great lengths to tell me just how desolate a place we were in. Taking my segment of parachute and a short length of parachute cord, I set about making my new home. It consisted of folding it over on itself, leaving a small entrance in which to feed your sleeping bag and climb through. Wes was most put out that my bivouac was far better than his was. He told me that he was going to destroy it in the middle of the night and claim that it fell to bits because it was so badly constructed. During the day, there was little else to do other than try different methods of trapping food and locating water. Wes was very good in his instruction and we soon had several traps and stills out. When it goes dark in the desert it is like someone

179

just switches the light off. One minute it is light the next it is dark. Not long after last light, and having seen no other sign of life at all, we all retired to our bashas. In the morning, I was pleased to see that Wes had not sabotaged my 'home'. He said that he had tried, but that it had been too dark to find it. I was very surprised to see that our camp area was covered with loads of different animal tracks ranging from snake tracks to camel footprints. No one had heard anything. It was a good job that a camel had not trodden on anyone during the night. The day was spent checking the different traps and snares from the day before, protecting ourselves from the sun by making headgear and sunglasses from carried items and making different types of shade to lower the temperature. These skills would be vital should I find myself in the unfortunate position of being on foot behind enemy lines. I have to say that there was little else to do during the daylight hours. Other than work out how to survive and navigate, we spent the time sheltering in our home made shade. The view out over the vast expanse of desert concerned me, as it was obvious that there would be little cover if I had to carry out escape and evasion drills. Not only that, I had not had much training or experience in that speciality and knew that if I had to do it for real, chances were that I would not make it back alive. Oh well, I thought, if you play big boys games, you play big boys rules.

That evening, as we were waiting for the sun to set, I was talking to Wes about how I felt regarding the possibility of a forthcoming conflict. I was a little concerned that I would be pushed to look after everybody, being that I was the only medic. He replied, matter of factly, that if the conflict started he did not expect all crews to survive and joked that it would help ease the numbers for me. It was one of those moments in your life when you really are unable to say something. I knew this wasn't an exercise and that all casualties would be real. It was quite probable that some of the crews, and the military units using the helicopters would not be going home. The thought left me feeling very uncomfortable. The silence between us seemed to last forever until it was broken by the ringing of the mobile telephone Wes had left in his basha. We looked towards each other and exchanged a glance as if to say, "This is it. We're at war." Wes jumped to his feet and sprinted to the ringing telephone. Everyone ran to be next to him in the hope that we would hear what was being said. "No mate.... No mate...... You've got the wrong number....... I'm not in the town.... I can't tell you where I am...... No mate, it's the wrong number." With that, Wes hit the button on the phone ending the call. He looked around at all of us and we burst out laughing. Here we were in the middle of absolutely nowhere, training for the worst case scenario of any military situation, and we get a wrong number!

The last day was spent evaluating whether or not our stills and traps had worked and breaking camp, leaving no trace of our having been there. I think we would have been very hungry and very thirsty had this been a 'live' situation. Although some of the stills had produced some water, it would not have been enough to keep all of us going. No one had caught anything edible either. In the real situation, it would be every man for himself. Not an encouraging thought.

With all bashas dismantled and all kit collected and packed ready to go, we sat waiting for the Chinook to collect us. Prior to us leaving for the survival exercise, arrangements had been made for a time to collect us. The Flight prided itself on being able to hit its infiltration or exfiltration point to within about five minutes of any prearranged time. As we waited, I could hear the familiar noise of the twin rotors. Looking around, it was very difficult to actually work out from which direction the noise was coming from. As the noise got louder, I saw the Chinook flying low and fast over the desert floor. Behind it was a feint dust trail caused by the downwash. We were at the top of a large plateau and I was looking down onto the helicopter as it approached head on. It pulled up directly in front of us and passed overhead at no more that ten feet. The noise was fantastic but we were sand blasted by the sand whipped up. The helicopter turned and landed a short distance away and we collected our kit and, after receiving the thumbs up from the rear loadmaster, ran up the back ramp into the helicopter. No sooner were we aboard, but the ramp was raised and the engine sound increased as the massive airframe lifted vertically. Turning back towards the way it had arrived, I looked out of the window at where our encampment had been. There was no trace of our existence. On the flight back I was lucky enough to get to sit in the jump seat. This is a canvas seat that is normally stowed against the wall in the narrow passageway leading into the cockpit. Once folded down the passenger sits in between and slightly behind both pilots. The view was fantastic but the seat was incredibly uncomfortable. I had a horrendous backache after the hour and a half flight back to Bateen. I didn't complain though, it had been worth it for the experience. On the way back, the crew had practised fast approaches to targets, tactical landings and takeoffs, navigation exercises and missile and radar avoidance drills. Never before had I been so impressed with flying skills. The individuals who flew on the Special Forces Flight were incredible. There was four to a crew – two pilots and two crewmen. They worked together as one. It was as if there was telepathy between them as they all appeared to know what the other would do next. The pilots, I am sure, were just a natural extension of the aircraft itself. I hoped that I would be able to be as professional at my job as these guys were at theirs.

On arrival back at Bateen, I made sure that I was available to anyone who wanted to see me for medical advice. There were not many takers. Everyone was taking care of themselves very well, with only the odd problem for me to solve. So far, so good.

Once the medical rounds were completed, I caught up on events that had occurred during my three days in the wilderness. I opened my mail and read all the newspapers that had been sent out by family back home. This always left you with mixed feelings. The pride that the Nation and your family were supporting you, but the horrible feeling of homesickness was ever present. Evening briefing informed us that additional crews were soon to arrive from the UK and that soon after that, we would be moving to a training area in the middle of nowhere. It was somewhere between Abu Dhabi and Dubai and was given the name Victor. This would be our training area, well away from prying eyes. The stakes had just gone up a level.

I spent the next few days reviewing my kit and equipment. I constantly wondered if I had enough supplies to cope with what lay ahead. One day I again disappeared into the desert with Wes Hogan. We had taken one of the SAS Land Rovers, affectionately referred to as a 'Pinkie' and were going to use it for extraction drills and underslung load flying. These Land Rovers were fantastic. They had tremendous acceleration and manoeuvrability. The plan had been for us to drive somewhere and await the arrival of one of the Chinooks to come and get us. Wes was driving as we were zooming across the flat desert roads. After a short stop, we decided that we would try and be awkward and go off track for a couple of hundred metres. Wes turned off the road and off we went. After about twenty metres we sank into the soft sand. We were stuck. As per the drills, we drove forwards and backwards in an attempt to free ourselves. There was about forty minutes before the Chinook arrived.

Changing gear from forwards to reverse and back again, we were getting nowhere and all the time the Land Rover was getting lower and lower in the sand. Looking side on to the vehicle, I noticed that the front wheels were going one way whilst the rear wheels were going in the opposite direction. The half-shaft had broken and we were going nowhere. There was nothing Wes and I could do so we sat about waiting for the Chinook to pick us up. I sat and wondered how the guys in the SAS would deal with such a situation like this. We could wait for a lift, but they would be miles behind enemy lines. The thought brought home to me exactly how serious this could all get so I did not dwell on it too much. Not only was there the embarrassment factor, but we had to return the vehicle to the SAS after having broken it in less than an hour. To be fair to them, they just looked to the heavens and accepted that we were idiots. The ribbing from the rest of the RAF however, was a different matter. The following day was Christmas Day. In order to beat the homesick blues, we all went to the hotel beach for a last party. Within the next 48 hours we would be moving to Victor. There were the odd one or two who kept saying that it may be their last Christmas, but on the whole everyone was fine.

On the last night in the hotel, Stumpy and I feasted on the mountain of complimentary chocolates that had been left on the pillow each night by the hotel staff. Not only that, each time we passed the maid's trolley I would help myself to a huge handful of chocolates from the basket and add them to our total. We had decided not to eat the chocolates, but to save them until our last night before moving into the field. I think we had about 20 each and both felt a little unwell at the end of our feast.

We finally moved to Victor on 28 December having been in the Abu Dhabi Intercontinental Hotel for a little over one month. It was a big culture shock. Victor was in the middle of nowhere and must have been left unoccupied for at least a few years. Although there were brick buildings, there was nothing inside them apart from layers of sand. It was back to camp beds and mozzie nets, and four or five to a room. The whole place needed cleaning from top to bottom and essential services such as the electricity and plumbing needed to be checked and repaired. The technicians set about fixing the services whilst the rest of us set about cleaning the place. A big difference between helicopter squadrons and fast jet squadrons is that the fast jet boys will always find themselves decent accommodation, leaving the ground crew behind in the mess, whereas helicopter crews always ended up in the mess with everyone else. This created a good bond between everyone.

The accommodation was eventually pronounced marginally fit for human habitation, although it needed regular cleaning parties to keep on top of everything. Sand would blow in and get everywhere, the toilets were the hole in the floor squat type, (which took a bit of getting used to), and insects were a major problem. The Special Forces Flight took over a small complex on the site with the SAS and SBS taking over similar complexes either side of us. The helicopters were a short distance away near to some recently acquired portacabins. The portacabins were to become the engineering office and flight line. My medical centre was near to the accommodation area and I spent the first day of 1991 sorting my kit, yet again.

The following day I met with the medics from the SAS and the SBS. The SAS had brought a doctor with them. I had worked with Captain Nick Groom in Hong Kong and thought he was a good doctor. Each SAS squadron had their own medic, a corporal from the RAMC, and there was a Staff Sergeant overseeing them. The SBS had two medics but no doctor. One of the SBS medics was a nineteen year old kid who had only recently finished his training. He was very excitable and was talking like he was personally going to walk to Baghdad and kill Saddam Hussain with his bare hands. I got on very well with the other SBS medic, a guy by the name of Larry Meek. He had been an SBS medic for many years and had delayed his discharge in order to finish his career 'with a bang.' I felt quite intimidated to be in the company of medics who had, I presumed, seen active service all over the world. Larry laughed it off saying that there would be no problem.

Orders came from on high that we were to start inoculating all troops with the anthrax vaccine, as there was a very real threat of biological and chemical warfare, should the talks fail. All medics met at the medical centre and a mass inoculation programme took place. There were one or two who absolutely refused to have the jabs, but on the whole everyone was vaccinated. The following day, medics included, everyone felt absolutely terrible. Arms ached, your body felt as though it weighed twice as much and you felt full of cold. Fortunately, the symptoms wore off after about 24 hours.

We were all now in what was called isolation. That meant we were not allowed to leave the Victor area for fear of compromising any operational issues. However, in order to obtain fresh rations, get bottled water and collect and deliver the post. One or two individuals were selected to act as runners, leaving the area on one or other of these tasks. I was fortunate enough to be one of those individuals.

There was one occasion I was on a post run, and had to go a small airfield in Dubai. As I watched the VC10 aircraft land, I saw a familiar face get off and head towards the main building. I quickly followed and finally caught up with my old friend. "Just what do you think you are doing here?" I

187

asked in my best aggressive tone. Sqn Ldr Evelyn Peters turned around. Her eyes widened and her mouth dropped open. I started laughing and we both just hugged. "What are you doing here?" she asked. I told her I was with a small RAF helicopter detachment and that I could not say any more. She was, as usual, extremely professional and asked no further questions although I am sure she knew exactly who I was working with. Evelyn had about 25 minutes in which to organise the collection of the patients she had come out to escort back to the UK, so unfortunately, our time together was short. Our meeting had given me a much needed morale boost. Prior to her boarding the aircraft again she gave me a kiss and said, "You are to take care and come home safely. That's an order!" It was the only kiss I had all war! Evelyn had said that she would telephone Pauline when she returned to the UK to say that we had met and that I was alright. I have no doubt it was the first thing she did after handing over her patients, and for that, Pauline and I will be eternally grateful.

The political talks were breaking down and everyone was getting a little tense. It was decided to hold a mass casualty exercise so that everyone could practice their role in such a situation. The patrol medics from both the SAS and SBS were given refresher training and the full time medics ran through our role. There was no way of transporting stretcher cases other than by carrying them, so I worked with one of the ground engineers to modify a short wheelbase Land Rover. Using angle iron as rails we were able to fit a rack on the back of the vehicle, which would allow us to slide stretchers on and off. The back of the Land Rover was lowered so that it could drive straight on and off a Chinook.

Everything was set and we waited for the exercise to start early the following morning. All medics were to be tested, so early in the morning the casualties were placed in and around the camp. At 07:30am the 'alarm' was sounded and the exercise was under way. I thought all eyes would be on me, as I was, in my mind, the only one that had not been tested under real battle conditions. I was directed to several casualties who had been caught in an explosion. One was seriously injured and after carrying out the priorities of first aid, I set up an intravenous infusion. This particular casualty was a SAS trooper. When I taped the end of the giving set to his arm he looked at me as if to say ' what good will that do?' He said, "We do it for real mate. That way we know if you can do your job." I felt both stupid and nervous. I had sited many infusions before, but if I were to mess this up, word would soon go around that the 'crab' medic was rubbish at his job. Fortunately, I managed to site it first time, more by luck I think.

My other casualties were walking wounded so as soon as they were patched up I began shouting for stretcher bearers. I could hear other medics also shouting, as well as their casualties. Some casualties always thought they were being assessed for an Oscar and would put their heart and soul into the part. Others would be quite bored by the whole experience. Fortunately for me I had mainly bored casualties. We had arranged for a Chinook to arrive at a designated collection point twenty minutes after the start of the exercise. It would wait for four minutes before lifting off. Anyone not on board would have to deal with the situation. Also, it would not look too good in front of all the others if I missed the ride. The majority of them were expected to go into enemy territory and would probably get themselves involved in some sort of conflict, or 'nonsense' as the SAS puts it. It would seriously undermine their confidence if the medical backup were not effective. I felt under tremendous pressure. However, the training kicked in and I felt as though I was working on autopilot. I soon had my casualties sorted out and arrived at the RV point with about one minute to spare before the arrival of the Chinook. The helicopter came in low and fast, landing some ten feet from where the main body of casualties and medics were waiting. The rear ramp came down and one of the loadmasters appeared, giving us the thumbs up to start loading. The right hand side of the Chinook had been rigged up to hold the stretcher cases, in three banks of three stretchers. These were loaded first starting at the front of the cabin working to the rear, and from top to bottom of each bank. As we were loading, the last group of casualties arrived. Thankfully, everyone had made the RV on time. Stretcher cases fully loaded, the walking wounded were led into the seats on the left hand side. When all seats were taken up, the remainder sat on the floor. Loading took just over the four minutes set and as the last medic boarded, the ramp was raised and the engine noise increased as the fully laden helicopter took to the air.

The flight to the American field hospital took about twenty minutes and there was a reception committee waiting for us when we landed. As all casualties were being transported on a RAF helicopter, I took responsibility as 'lead medic'. Not for any other reason than this was my speciality. I nominated the most 'severe' cases and had them unloaded first, followed by the not so serious, with the walking wounded following on behind. The Americans were very professional. The hospital was well organised and able to cater for the influx of patients. Our 'patients' were whisked off to the relevant departments for examination and treatment. All of a sudden there was a shout from one of the treatment cubicles. "Doc, come here. This one's really injured!" I followed into the cubicle to be faced with a concerned nurse and a bemused SAS trooper. The nurse had undone the bandage on the trooper to find that the infusion drip really was in place. They had assumed that the patient was genuinely injured. When I explained that no one was really injured, the medical staff could not understand why the drips had been used. "So everyone gets the practice." was my reply. I could tell that they were very confused.

After the exercise was called to an end, everyone made their way back to the front of the hospital. The only question that was now asked by the Americans was, "Exactly who are you guys?" We had expected this question, so everyone had used the cover story that we were a small British Army signals unit. Once back on board the Chinook, we took off and made the journey back to Victor. The de-brief went well and I was pleased that, in my own mind, I had proved myself to these hardened veterans. The only slight issue was the second medic attached to the SBS. As I said, he was a young lad who had just completed his training before being posted in. He was incredibly keen, but too much so for the SBS' liking. He was talking along the lines of winning the war on his own. What he was going to do when he got hold of Saddam Hussain wasn't worth mentioning. His medical skills were fine; it was his gung-ho attitude that was a problem.

Unbeknown to me, the senior officers of the SBS were expressing concern about their young medic. They had approached our Flight Commander, Squadron Leader Steve French, to ask if he would allow me to be the second SBS medic. I was duly called into the office and offered the position. I accepted immediately and hoped that the flutter of nerves didn't show too much. What was I letting myself in for? My acceptance resulted in the young medic being sent back to the UK. I felt a little guilty, but also very flattered. In the days that followed, I was included in the practices of infiltration and extraction. What an eye opener! I was also very pleased that I had undertaken the desert survival training. That said, I accepted the fact that should I end up on foot, on the wrong side of any battle line, my chances of survival would be slim to say the least. I knew I was nowhere near ready, but I would give it a good go.

On 16 January we were told to make ourselves ready for a move. Make sure you have enough kit for about two weeks was the other instruction. We are going onto hard rations.
This was it, I thought. The forward move. However, I still didn't grasp the fact that in less than 24 hours we would be at war. That realisation would come with the dawn of a new day.

Chapter 10

As I awoke next morning, the whole camp was bustling. Word was going around that the war had started. Coalition forces had begun a massive air assault on key military and industrial sites. Everyone made their way to the dining room for breakfast. However, when all were seated, and those left were standing around the edge of the room, a shout for quiet settled everyone down. An Army Officer then climbed onto one of the dining tables and began preparing to address all who were assembled. It was going to be one of those morale building, fighting spirit type speeches, I thought. The Officer turned out to be Colonel Sir Michael Rose, Director of the Special Forces. Sir Michael had been the Commanding Officer of the SAS during both the Iranian Embassy siege and the Falklands conflict, and had been instrumental in negotiating the Argentine surrender. In the few moments before he addressed us all, I tried to savour the moment. Here I was, a simple RAF medic in with the elite of the British Armed Forces, on the first day of war. It was the largest gathering of Special Forces personnel since the Second World War.

"Gentlemen," came the obligatory opening. A hush settled in the room. " I should come out with some wonderful stirring speech on the morning of this momentous occasion. However, let me just tell you this little story. I was in the mess having breakfast the other morning and I sat at a table where there was a Scots Guards officer. I noticed that he was wearing his hat. A short while after I had sat down, I asked him if he could pass the salt and pepper. He ignored me, so I asked him again. He continued to ignore me so I tapped him on the arm and again asked for the salt and pepper. The Guards officer turned toward me and said, "When a Guards officer wears his head dress at the dining table it means he does not wish to be disturbed!" I pushed my chair back, used it to climb onto the table and walked through his breakfast to get the salt and pepper. After I had got down from the table, I said to him, when a SAS officer asks you to pass the salt and pepper, it means pass the f****** salt and pepper!"

Everyone erupted in laughter. Sir Michael stood there waiting for the silence to return. He concluded his speech with comments about everyone being the elite of the British Armed Forces and that we should be proud of our opportunity to be involved in such an historic event. He made reference to the SAS returning to the desert – the location of their humble beginnings in World War 2, before climbing down from the table to rapturous applause. He was right, I did feel proud. A little scared, but proud. I would do my utmost to look after the people in my care.

Breakfast over, word went around that we would be moving to our forward operating base the following day and that we should collect what equipment we would need for a two week period. Yet again I had to guess how much, and what kind of equipment and medication I would need. This time, however, it was for real. I took as much as possible, leaving all other kit in metal lacon containers at Victor, hoping I wouldn't need it as a re-supply. I spent the remainder of the day packing, unpacking and re-packing kit. By the end of the day, my kit was sat inside the oblong chalk mark on the hangar floor waiting for loading onto one of the Hercules transport aircraft that would fly us to our forward operating base. It was reported to be only 100 kilometers (60 miles) from the Saudi Iraqi border. We were to have an overnight stop at the King Falid International Airport in Saudi Arabia, before moving on to our final destination.

Later that afternoon we boarded the Hercules for the short flight to KFIA. The airport itself was very busy, and because of the nature of our involvement, we were not allowed to wander around the area. We spent our time in a partly built construction that had about half an inch of dust and sand on the floor. The mixture of sand and concrete dust made it look like we were living on the surface of the moon. We set up our small camp beds, made a cup of tea and had something to eat from our ration packs. Not the best restaurant in the area, but under the circumstances it would have to do. There was very little for us to do, so after the sun had set, most of us climbed into our sleeping bags and tried to sleep. It was difficult as there were aircraft taking off and landing all through the night.

The next morning arrived after what appeared to be a long restless night. After a breakfast of rolled oats, it was down to the airfield to help load all kit onto the Hercules and Chinooks. No sooner was everything on board, everyone was told to get their personal kit and board themselves. I was on one of the Special Forces Hercules. The regulations were a little relaxed as I climbed on top of a pile of boxes lashed to the floor with netting. I was wearing my flying helmet and just lay back on the top of the freight. I pulled down the visor, without removing the cloth visor cover and closed my eyes. The noise of the four engines combined with the vibration of the whole airframe soon had me drifting off into a deep sleep. I recall the start of the taxiing but remember little else about the flight. Here I was, flying to within 60 miles of the enemy's border and I was sleeping like a log. I didn't realise how tired I was. I next recall being kicked awake by the Hercules Loadmaster. As I sat up, lifted the visor up and tried to remember where I was. The Loadmaster grunted something about coming into land. This place, wherever it was, would be my home for the next seven weeks, although at that time I had no idea how long it would be, even though I had not believed the original estimation of two weeks. I also wondered whether everyone who was making the trip this way would be fortunate enough to make the return journey. I desperately prayed that that would be the case.

As we touched down I looked out of one of the small windows. Sand was blowing everywhere. The back ramp of the Hercules began to lower and more sand blew in along with the now familiar warm air. The noise of the propellers increased and the Hercules ground to a halt. Like a well-oiled, but now sandy machine, everyone set about unloading all the kit. We were met by the small advanced party, who told us where everything would be going. Our new home was a desert airfield called Al Jouf, some 100km from the Iraqi border. Our homes were a line of 12' by 12' tents and the Operations Room was the small airport building. The engineering area was on the other side of the airfield. Also moving in were the SAS Squadrons and the SBS marines, although they tended to keep themselves to themselves. It was decided that the aircrew would allocate accommodation as per each crew, with all ground crew mixing and matching. I would be sharing with two engineers, one supply NCO and the Ops SNCO Stan Young. I became great mates with Stan and also one of the engineers, a pseudo Australian called Don Sparks, and I have to say that over the coming weeks, both would play a great part in keeping me sane.

Life was very much the same as when we were at Victor, except for the fact that we were now living in tents. The only hard buildings were a small airport arrivals and departure block, some (very) basic Arabic squat type toilets and a building on the far side of the airfield that was taken over by the engineers as their workshop. Apart from that... just sand. Al Jouf was a small airfield in the middle of nowhere and was only used by the Saudis in exceptional circumstances. This was obviously one of those circumstances. There had been a small advanced party arrive the day before us and they had set up the accommodation tents prior to the arrival of everyone else. This was a great relief as everyone was so tired after the last move. I would reckon that the majority had managed about 3-4 hours sleep out of the previous 48 hours, and most were ready for collapsing. Including me, despite sleeping on the Hercules flight.

I was always concerned about moving to a new location and worried about things such as did everyone know where to find me in an emergency, did I have the right equipment, where was my nearest medical backup and (as was constantly in my mind) could I hack it if the going got tough? Tiredness was now catching up with me. I made sure that I had set up my medical kit in what was designated the Medical Centre area and that I had told everyone which tent I would be in. It had been decided prior to our move that we would now start taking the nerve agent protection tablets called NAPS. One tablet was to be taken every eight hours. It was supposed to offer protection to the nervous system in the event of a nerve agent attack, as there was genuine concern that Saddam Hussain may use chemical weapons. There were various rumors knocking about with regard to these tablets and some people elected not to take theirs. As I was the medical representative advocating the health protection methods, I felt that I should set an example and take mine. It was some two hours before my next NAPS tablet was due, but I was too tired to stay up in order to take it on time. I took the tablet, crawled into my sleeping bag and almost immediately fell into a much-needed deep sleep. My next recollection was being shaken awake by one of the engineers. He looked wide-eyed and was in a state of minor panic. "Brian, Brian!" he shouted. Dragging myself out of a coma, I asked what the problem was. The engineer told me that he had taken his NAPS tablets and tried to go to sleep. As he was trying to get to sleep, his body jerked itself awake. In a panic, he thought he was having some sort of reaction to the tablets and that his Central Nervous System was now shot to bits. I looked at my watch. I had been asleep for 30 minutes. I quietly checked him over – blood pressure, pulse, pupils etc and reassured him that it was one of those occasions where the body had fallen asleep before the brain, and it was the brain's way of waking the body up. Not surprising really, due to the previous 24 hours we had had. He took a little convincing before he went away and I retreated to my sleeping bag. I don't remember much else until the next morning.

That next morning soon arrived and everyone was up fairly early, walking around trying to orientate themselves with the new site. It was a small purpose built civilian airport in the middle of nowhere. The airport was not a regularly used site so although there were several members of the Saudi armed forces, no one else was aware of our location. This would be home for the next seven weeks. My first full day was spent finding a suitable location to have as a medical centre area. There were very few available buildings as most had been taken over by the Operations department and, naturally, access to that particular area was restricted. Eventually, I settled for the lean-to area of a small white building, the main part of which was used by the safety equipment guys. It wasn't a very big area to work in, and there was no door and the walls were built with airbrick thereby allowing a good view into the medical area. One of my little foibles has always been that of confidentiality and the confidentiality of my patients was paramount to me. I wasn't happy with the location available, but there was nowhere else for me to go. Not only that, but I was expected to leave all my equipment there, even if I was away from the building. Well, I thought, if they want to steal the very kit that may be needed to save their own lives that was their problem. Not so much as a plaster was taken without my knowledge. My concerns were completely unfounded.

Our rations consisted of the good old-fashioned 24 hour ration packs. That small cardboard box full of small tins of tasteless food and out of date chocolate. We heated the food using the small hexamine blocks that went with the 'rat packs'. The tins were heated in boiling water and the water then used to make a good old English cuppa. Our second evening at Al Jeuf saw me boiling up my water for the evening meal. Everyone in the tent agreed that in order to preserve rations, we would have a communal drink of tea after the meal. This saved tea bags and also hexamine blocks. The water had boiled and the food was eaten. It was my turn to make the tea so I threw two of the precious tea bags into the water and stirred. At that point, the air raid siren sounded. There are always those one or two seconds of reaction time to a new situation. A quick look at each other and then it was into the personal protection drills. Usually, when back in the UK we had training in these drills once a year. Very few of us ever listened. However, prior to leaving the UK we had been given an extra brief. I had heard every word. As quickly as possible, we all began to dress ourselves in the full personal protection equipment. Respirator, NBC suit, gloves and boots. It was a tense time. There was a very real threat that Saddam Hussain would use chemical or biological weapons. Once dressed, we paired off and checked each other to make sure there were no gaps in our clothing. After that we all sat on out beds just looking at the tea, steaming away and getting colder by the minute. There was a discussion as to whether we should go outside and stand in the small trenches to the rear of the line of tents, but we all agreed that having the cover of the tent was better protection against chemical droplets and vapour that nothing at all. Had this been an exercise back in the UK, we would have all left off our respirators and drunk the tea. As it was, no one was volunteering to take their respirator off to see if it was OK. About 45 minutes later the all clear sounded. The tea was cold. It was decided that someone else would make a new brew as I was probably jinxed. Stranger things had happened!

A few days later, on January 22nd 1991, 7 Squadron Special Forces Flight finally flew its first mission into enemy territory. The task involved flying a number of SBS guys to a location some 60 kilometers from Baghdad. I volunteered to go along as a medic, but was refused permission by the SBS Major. After flying for a few hours along a pre-planned route, weaving in and around known threats, the Chinook finally arrived at the designated landing area. The SBS left the back of the helicopter and disappeared into the darkness of the night to dig up a length of fibre optic cable, believed to be part of a scud missile communication system, and then fill the hole in so that no one knew where the break in the line was. The Chinook was sat on the ground with its rotors turning, for about 2 hours whilst the SBS did their thing. After the war, I think the SBS mounted the cable on a plaque and presented it to General Schwarzcopf. The Chinook pilot was rightly awarded the Distinguished Flying Cross for his planning and execution of such a daring sortie. I can remember lying awake in my sleeping bag waiting to hear the sound of the Chinook return. It seemed like forever until the familiar sound of the rotors thundered overhead. After a low pass over the campsite, the Chinook finally landed and shut down its engines. Relieved, I drifted off to sleep.

In the morning, everyone was on a high. The previous night's mission had been a high-risk operation. The SBS were the first into action and I got the impression that that hadn't sat well with the SAS. Nevertheless, it had been a 7 Squadron Chinook that had transported the guys into enemy territory. I was pleased to find Larry safe and well, as I had struck up quite a good relationship with him following my so-called secondment to the SBS. Not only that, he had taken some of my medical kit with him and I wanted it back! The following couple of days saw missions prepared and scrubbed at the last minute. I had been warned for one or two and have to admit that I felt quite scared at the thought of flying miles behind enemy lines. In the end, the flights never went. My main task now was to convince everyone to have the follow up Anthrax and plague jabs. Not an easy task following the number of sore arms and flu like symptoms that occurred last time. Also, there was another lottery draw for one of the crewmen to give me my jabs. The draw was rigged and the honour, again, fell to Wes Hogan as he had done such a good job of it the last time and I wasn't about to let any of the others get their own back.

Strange as it may seem, a large square of Astroturf appeared from somewhere on the airfield complex. It had been spotted a few days earlier and a plan had been hatched to 'liberate' it. Following the second successful military operation by 7 Squadron, we duly laid it on the floor of the tent. At last something other than sand to walk on. We had the only lawned accommodation in the Gulf – luxury! There were a lot of visitors to the tent in the next few days just to see if the rumors were true.

Thankfully, there was little for me to do medically at this time. I had realised that most of the work we would be carrying out would be done in the darkness of night. How would I see my patient if I had to treat them in the back of the helicopter? I set about manufacturing a light proof tent that would fit around a bank of stretchers. This project took me several days to complete. I cut up a 9' x 9' tent and hand stitched most of the parts together. Rope was attached to the tent so that it could be secured to the cabin of the aircraft. After a few modifications, it worked! I was delighted. There were a great deal of possibilities for using this piece of equipment but for the time being, a light proof casualty treatment area would have to do. The Special Forces aircrew were particularly impressed. I felt very proud of my achievements. I was quite prepared to take this into enemy territory, safe in the knowledge that I would be able to do my best for the casualty. Fortunately, it was never tested in anger. Selfishly, I was a little disappointed that I was not given the opportunity to put it to use.

A few days later, I was placed on standby to go on a recovery flight, deep into Iraq. I rigged the tent and put the medical equipment I thought I might need inside the tent. I also prepared my personal equipment. I stripped and cleaned my SA80 rifle, made sure that my webbing had fresh water and some food on it somewhere. I also made sure that I had my escape and evasion map, gold sovereigns and 'goolie chit' somewhere about my person. The 'goolie chit' was a document written in English and Arabic, promising that the British Government would pay the sum of £5000 to anyone helping a British serviceman escape. Each 'chit' was individually numbered so that identifications could be made at a later date. You also had to hand in a sealed envelope containing personal information, known only to you. This information would be used in the event of a rescue. In order to eliminate the possibility of a false rescue message being sent you would be questioned on the content of the envelope. In addition there was a two-part phrase. The rescuers gave the first part and the rescuee gave the reply. As I was a medic, I decided my phrase would be – "Take two Aspirin", with the reply being – "And see me in the morning". In the end the flight was scrubbed at the last moment and I was told to be ready to go the following night. That too was scrubbed at the last minute, so I never did get to go on an operational mission behind enemy lines. It was only later that I found out that these two flights were rescue attempts for the missing Bravo Two Zero mission. As there had been no radio contact from them, it was decided by those higher up the food chain to be too much of a risk for the helicopter and aircrew. I still have no doubt to this day that the skill of the crews could have pulled the mission off successfully. Still, it was not their decision to make. I knew that they wanted to go and get their own men back.

Several days later, I flew to a French Foreign Legion hospital at a place called Rafha. An SAS trooper had been shot whilst behind the lines in Iraq. In order to get their injured friend to hospital, the remaining members of the team had hijacked a car and driven across the desert until they found this place. On arrival in the town, the local police treated them as hostile, until one of the team had the bright idea of offering the stolen car as a gift to the senior police officer present. Happy with his new car, the policeman took the team to the hospital, where emergency surgery was performed on the injured man. He had been shot in the stomach and the bullet had nicked his liver. It was my job to assess whether or not he would be fit to fly back to the UK for further treatment. As it was, he still had a drain in situ and his blood count was quite low. I said that he was not fit to move for about another week, so would have to stay where he was. At that time he was posted as 'missing in action'. His family would have been made aware of that fact, so the injured soldier desperately wanted a message sending back to his family telling them that he was all right. The Colonel of the Regiment decided that this could not be done due to operational security, however I do know that his family received a very quick and cryptic call around the time I was off base collecting fresh rations. About one week later, the soldier was on his way back home. He was replaced on the team by the Sergeant Major I had walked out to the burning Galaxy aircraft with, right at the start of the deployment. By all accounts he was a ferocious man.

It soon became apparent that we could be at Al Jouf for quite a long time. I had been there for three weeks, permanently on call for any emergency or mission. A decision was taken to start sending people back to Victor for a few days R&R. I would be on the second batch, with Larry covering all medical emergencies. When it was my turn to fly back to Victor, I was walking towards the ramp of the Hercules when I saw a few SAS soldiers walking in the same direction. In the middle of them was a small man, no boots and a sandbag over his head. He was being guided to the aircraft by the barrel of an M16 carbine. I was going to be flying back with a POW. As I approached the ramp, it was indicated that I should not speak, and just take a seat on the red netting bench along the cabin wall. The Iraqi soldier was directed to the other side of the cabin. A strange memory, but to this day I can still recall his bright red football socks. I felt a little sorry for him, although was not worried about his well being as I knew that although he would get a thorough debriefing, he would be well looked after. Unlike any of our guys!

To my knowledge, he was the only prisoner taken by the Special Forces throughout the whole campaign. I remembered the lyrics from one of my favourite songs sung by Bette Midler. The song was 'From a distance' and the line went: *From a distance you look like my friend, even though we are at war.* On the aircraft, I lay down, intending to sleep my way back to Victor.

Flight back to Victor over, I now had two days to myself. I caught up with my letter writing and managed to get into the local town. I phoned home and spoke to Pauline, which left me feeling absolutely brilliant. One of the lads at Victor had written home every day and that had got some of us into trouble with our wives. Pauline had asked why this lad's wife had received a letter almost every day while she got about one a week. I hadn't told her that we had moved to the Forward Operating Base so explained the letter shortage by telling her it was boring and nothing happened to write about. I tried to increase the letter writing though, in between everything else.

All too soon I was back on a Hercules heading for my grassy tent in Al Jewf. The day after I arrived back in Al Jewf I was on the weapon ranges. I watched an awesome demonstration of firepower by the SAS, and then stepped up with my meager SA80. It was soon apparent that it did not work too well. Stoppage after stoppage soon put paid to my time on the range. Back in the tent, I took my rifle to pieces and thoroughly cleaned and greased the moving parts. I thought that I had been doing well in keeping it clean, put obviously I had not. A valuable lesson had been learnt.

During the day, most of the groundcrew, when not working, would try to get some sleep. It was difficult due to the heat (although at night it was difficult due to the cold!). However, what made it more difficult was that most of the SBS would sit around making loads of noise either with their music systems or just being generally quite noisy. They were still buoyant after their outstanding mission. I could see most of the groundcrew getting more than a little fed up with not being able to sleep, so I did what many called either very brave or very foolish. I told them all to shut up. I reminded the SBS guys that the people who looked after the helicopters they might use in enemy territory were having difficulty in getting any rest. I also said that tired people tended to make mistakes and that they could draw whatever inference they wanted to. My advice was to go and be noisy elsewhere. I expected to either get my head kicked in or to watch the SBS move elsewhere. Fortunately it was the latter.

The following days were spent around the campsite maintaining the health of the RAF guys and sweeping out tons of sand following a particularly severe sandstorm. There was always movement in and out of the camp, either by helicopter or by vehicles. There were stories that on one of the recent SAS re-supply runs 80 odd miles inside Iraqi territory, a full Warrant Officer and SNCO Mess meeting was held, and that a decision to buy new chairs had been agreed on. The chairman of the Mess Committee had also agreed to eat the minutes of the meeting in the event of him being involved in a 'nonsense' - the SAS term for a firefight, prior to him returning to Al Jewf. Such class! There was also news that an SAS trooper had been killed in action. Although we knew of the patrol 'missing in action', this was the first confirmed soldier killed in action. It was a horrible feeling, even though I didn't know him. A Chinook was tasked to go and retrieve the trooper's body from inside Iraq. I asked if I would be allowed to go on the flight, as I would like to wash, clean and prepare the body of the soldier, so that he would look a little more presentable upon arrival back at the camp. I don't know why I wanted to do this, but I just did. I think it was a sign of respect for someone who made the ultimate sacrifice. I was disappointed when my request was turned down. The reason given that it was an unnecessary risk to take me along. I argued that it was a risk I was prepared to take but was told by Sqn Ldr French that I would not be going. I held Sqn Ldr French in high regard so, reluctantly, accepted his decision.

A few days later, on 24th February 1991, the ground offensive started. The conflict moved rapidly after that. Again, there were troop movements in and out of the camp, both by air and by road. During this time, we had been well forward of the main forces, but as the ground offensive gained momentum, other units began to move up to our location. An American unit arrived. They don't travel light! There was a huge mess areas with a menu that had choices other than take it or leave it. To be fair, our chefs had been absolutely magnificent. With limited provisions they had managed to feed us all with palatable and sustaining meals. I had no complaints at all, but it was nice to have a wider selection of food. Fresh stuff too! In addition to the food, the Americans brought with them a complete shower facility. Luxury! I could now have a wash in hot water. With my clothes, webbing and SA80 just outside of the water splash area, I was stark naked and covered in hot soapy water for the first time in ages. All of a sudden there was a huge explosion and sand flying everywhere. I quickly dived out of the shower and ran down the road to the medical centre area, dressing as I ran, putting my webbing on and dragging my SA80 as best I could. I thought, "Great". Someone will be telling my wife "I'm sorry Mrs Dixon. Your husband died stark naked and covered in soapsuds. He was a hero!"

On arrival at the main accommodation area, I was told that the explosion had been caused by an American A10 Thunderbolt flying nearby. It had developed some sort of problem and ditched its payload in the desert rather close to where we were. Fortunately, no one had been injured. After that excitement, the days passed quite uneventfully, until the point where the Iraqi military surrendered. Thank goodness!

One of the Chinooks was tasked to fly to Kuwait. Its mission was to fast rope SBS marines onto the British Embassy to ensure that it was safe for reoccupation. I was asked if I would like to go along as the second medic to Larry. I jumped at the chance. However, the day before the flight left, I was called into the SBS Commanding Officers office and told that I was not being allowed to go. When I protested, he told me that it was not because he doubted my medical skills, it was because

I was not counter-terrorist trained and would, therefore, be too much of a risk. Again, my protests were refused. I was bitterly disappointed. The mission went ahead and was a great success. Pictures of the SBS fast roping into the embassy were transmitted throughout the world, and printed in many newspapers.

Less than a week later, I was on the Iraqi border watching a long line of SAS Land Rovers, known as 'pinkies' return from enemy territory. They had been behind enemy lines for five weeks. I felt a great deal of pride watching their safe return. I knew that I was well down in the food chain of the Special Forces, but I felt that I had played my part and 'done my bit'. I was very proud to have been associated with them and to witness history in the making, even though, as I thought at the time, the majority of this history would remain untold. Once the long train of vehicles was safely back over the border, we all returned to the camp at Al Jewf. It was a great feeling.

The final highs and lows for me at Al Jewf were the news that the missing SAS patrol had been accounted for, but unfortunately three of them had been killed. Again, I felt a great sadness for them. I was also proud to be in the audience when General 'Stormin' Norman Schwarzcopf paid us a visit. After his speech to the 'magnificent British Special Forces' I felt ten feet tall, despite, as I have already said, being quite low down in the food chain.

As with all things Special Forces, once the job has been completed, arrangements are made to get all troops out of the area as quickly as possible. One more night would be spent at Al Jewf before moving back to Abu Dhabi, via Victor to make sure everything was packed. Strange as it sounds, I was quite sad to leave the following day.

Three days later, I began my flight home in a Hercules. There were five of us ready to go. The Hercules was a 'normal' one and not one of the Special Forces ones. Of the five of us on the flight, three were RAF and two were SAS. I was placed in charge of the passengers. About an hour prior to take off, the pilot came down the front steps and announced that the aircraft was too heavy and that we would not be going home. He was quite a young man, who looked too fresh to have been in the region for any length of time. On the other hand, we all looked rather disheveled with our long hair and tatty combats. One of the SAS guys was a scouser by the name of Joe. He was a huge man. Joe took hold of the pilot by the neck and lifted him up the side of the aircraft. Now looking up at the pilot, he said, "I've told my family that I'm going home today. If I don't go home, I'm going to kill you. I don't mean hit you and hurt you, I mean I'll take you out in the desert and kill you."
Joe then released his grip and the pilot returned to the ground, before scurrying back up the steps from whence he had come. Joe turned and winked at us. A few moments later, the quartermaster of the SAS drove a forklift truck out to the Hercules and unloaded one of the pallets containing stores. After the forklift had left, the pilot re-emerged and announced that we would now all be going home after all. Joe climbed on board and strung up his hammock in the gap left by the missing pallet.

Crafty git, I thought. As we taxied out to the runway, I had some sleeping tablets and passed them out to any of the passengers who wanted them, before taking one myself and settling down to sleep away the first leg of the flight that would take us to Cyprus.

I woke up about five minutes out from Cyprus feeling fine. Joe was in his hammock reading a book. "Tablet didn't do too much Brian", he said. "I need some sleep between here and home or I'll have to sort you out!" Oh dear I thought. Anyway, we taxied to a halt and we all got off the aircraft to stretch our legs. Joe saw a minibus and decided that he would like to go to the mess to get something to eat. We all thought this was a good idea so we just jumped in and drove off before anyone had the chance to say we couldn't. It was about 10.00am when we found the mess. When we went in the chef looked at us and started moaning about it being mid morning and that we were too late for breakfast and too early for lunch. Joe leant over the servery and took hold of the chef's neckerchief. Pulling the chef's head down towards the hotplate, he said very quietly "My name is Mr Hungry, and Mr Hungry would like some food!"

After being let go, the chef stood up, realised his mistake and probably correctly guessed which unit Joe was from. He told us all to take a seat and then began supplying us with all the food we could eat. I was so pleased I was on a flight with Joe! Suitably refreshed, we returned in the stolen minibus to the waiting Hercules and re-boarded ready to make the final leg of the flight home. Again I passed around the sleeping tablets, but this time told Joe to take two or three. I knew it would be safe, as he was as big as a mountain!

I woke up about ten minutes out from RAF Lyneham, in Wiltshire. Fortunately for me, Joe had managed to get some sleep. I would survive the war after all! After landing and following handshakes all round, the SAS guys went their way and the RAF guys boarded the transport back to RAF Odiham, where a small welcoming party waited for us at the Squadron hangar. The Senior Medical Officer, Sqn Ldr de Banner, met me off the coach. He was a man for whom I had the utmost respect. A kind and considerate man, and an excellent doctor. Sqn Ldr de Banner drove me home after I had finished my glass of champagne. My war was over, and I was delighted to be back home. However, my thoughts were, and always will be, with those who did not return.

Chapter 11

After a week off, I was back at work in the medical centre. The priority was collecting and restocking my medical boxes in case the Squadron was deployed at short notice. I had to take the ambulance to the Squadron hangar to bring all my lacon containers and extra kit back. There was sand everywhere!

However, I was finding it difficult to settle back into the daily routine of 'normal' RAF life. I noticed that I was more 'snappy' than I had been before going to the Gulf. The staff in the medical centre were brilliant, putting up with me and accepting that there would be a period of adjustment for me. Without doubt they all helped me to readjust back into normal life. I think those of us who had been in the Gulf all felt fairly similar. There was a network of people 'dropping in' for impromptu tea breaks, during which the topic of discussion was always the settling back into normal life, and how boring military life now was. There was never the 'been there – done that' attitude, but it was strange working without the constant adrenaline rush. It must have been difficult for Pauline too. I had been away for just under 5 months before returning and upsetting both her and Mark's daily routine. As always, she never complained and took everything in her stride. People have often said that one of the hardest jobs in the world is that of a Service wife. I would have to agree!

To add insult to injury, the MoD decided that I had been paid too much 'water allowance' whilst away in the Gulf, and promptly docked the princely sum of £180.00 from my pay. I had actually paid to go to war!

Life carried on as normal, with everyone settling back down within a few months. I had heard that there was due to be a Squadron deployment to RAF Valley in the not too distant future. There was no need for them to take a medic as RAF Valley had a fully equipped medical centre on the base. However, I was bored at work and persuaded the Flight Commander, Steve French, that I should be taken along. I think he took pity on me and agreed to let me go. The preparation was easy, as I knew that if I had forgotten anything, I could always get it from the RAF Valley medics. This would be an easy week away, and indeed it was. The detachment commander was Flight Lieutenant Rick Cook. Rick was a great bloke and I have very fond memories of sharing a beer or two with him, talking until the wee small hours. Tragically, Rick would lose his life in the Mull of Kintyre crash on 2 June 1994 along with fellow pilot, Flight Lieutenant Jonathan Tapper and crewmen Master Air Loadmaster Graham Forbes and Sergeant Kevin Hardie. Graham and Kev had also served in the Gulf War. All four were excellent people.

On arrival at Valley, I located the best place for the medical centre and dumped all my kit. I then, as usual, helped set up the rest of the site. Despite the fact that we were on a RAF base, the Special Forces Flight always had accommodation well away from the main areas of whichever base we were at. Even the meals were collected from the mess and brought to where we were. This all helped with operational security. The less we mixed with others, the less chance there was that one of the tasks could be compromised. Even when we were training, we adopted this set-up, as all training was made to be as real as possible. One thing I always did, when staying on a RAF Base, was to go to the Station Medical Centre and introduce myself to the SNCO in charge, and the Doctor. This was out of courtesy and also to let them know that they may get the odd emergency through the door, depending on how the training went! Imagine my surprise when I found out that the SNCO was none other than Sgt Ivor Fuller, my old sergeant from RAF Kinloss. What a small world. I remembered that he had telephoned me up not long after the Gulf War finished and asked whether or not the rumor of me being with the SAS was true. I reminded him that he was talking to me on an insecure telephone system and that not all rumors were true. Now here I was, in his medical centre telling him that there was a detachment from the Special Forces Flight, on the same station! He was like someone possessed. Gathering round all his staff he advised them that the subject was not to be discussed outside of the building under pain of being jailed in the guardroom. His complete over-reaction reminded me of his performance at RAF Kinloss, and proved to me that he hadn't changed!

I eventually left the medical centre and went back to the detachment location, happy that the medical backup was there should I need it. As a thank you, I managed to get several of the medics a trip on one of the Chinooks. The week passed without event and we were all soon back into the daily routine at RAF Odiham. I was getting more and more restless. I was unsure of my future, but I was sure that I didn't want to spend the rest of my time cooped up in a Medical Centre. I was extremely happy doing the job I was doing, but I knew it wouldn't last forever. I thought about taking a commission, but I was too young for a branch commission (you had to be aged 35, and I was 28) and I did not have the academic qualifications to allow me to take the quicker, more direct route to a commission. Deep down, I knew the end was in sight.

I began looking around outside to see what jobs were on offer. The ambulance service was a non-starter because of the low salary that they offered. Eventually, I settled for the police service. After successfully completing all entrance examinations and fitness tests, I was offered a place in the Hampshire Constabulary. I took the latest available date – 7 December 1992 and applied for discharge by purchase from the RAF. This meant that I paid them another sum of money, and they let me leave. It was to cost me £200 and they agreed to let me go on the 6th December 1992.

However, in the remaining time I had in the RAF, another deployment was planned. It was a training exercise with D Squadron SAS, the boat troop specialists. The exercise would be in October, would last a week and would be based in the south of France. On the morning of the deployment, I set off from home on my motorbike, with my bergen, full of kit, slung on my back. As I travelled along the road at about 45 miles an hour, the rear wheel of my bike locked causing me to skid. I was skidding into the path of oncoming traffic but managed to somehow steer the bike away from the traffic, back onto my side of the road. At some point, the bike and I parted company. When I had finished tumbling, I was relieved to find out that I was not seriously injured. I had, however, dislocated my left shoulder. Realizing that if I didn't do something fairly quickly, the muscles in my shoulder would go into spasm, I grabbed hold of a tree and yanked my shoulder back into place. It hurt like Hell, but fortunately it worked. I looked at my bike and realised that it was going no further so I started thumbing a lift along the side of the road. I wasn't being big and tough, it was just that there was no way I was going to miss my last ever deployment! Thankfully a kind motorist gave me a lift the rest of the way to RAF Odiham. I wasn't feeling too bad at that point. I telephoned Pauline to let her know what had happened and that I was OK. I asked her to make arrangements to get the bike collected from the side of the road and told her that I would sort everything out when I got back into the UK. As usual, she was fantastic. I then saw the doctor and asked that he just check over my shoulder to make sure everything was OK. He was more bothered about my bike so I went to the dispensary and helped myself to a handful of Brufen, a musco-skeletal painkiller. I thought it would be enough to deal with the pain until we got to our destination, and I could then sort myself out properly. It was about half an hour prior to the time we were due to leave for France. Throwing a few of the tablets down my throat, I left the medical centre and walked off down to the Squadron hangar ready for departure.

Dumping my bergen on arrival, I checked to make sure that all my medical kit was loaded. A short while later, all personnel who were going on the deployment made their way onto one of the two Chinooks and sat on the red webbing seat which runs along the edge of each side of the cabin. Running along the centre of the floor was all the equipment that would be needed for the trip. To say it was cramped would be an understatement! The flight lasted just over an hour and, for the first time ever in a helicopter, I was sick. This was quite annoying, as the flight was as smooth as you could expect from a Chinook. I told everyone it was delayed shock from the motorbike accident and I still believe this to be the case.

On arrival at the French Army conscript's camp, we unloaded everything into the accommodation block. The building was borderline condemned. The windows were hanging off, there was no electricity and it was full of rats. There were rooms full of bunk beds with the thinnest of mattresses. I took one of the top bunks and immediately regretted it as the whole bunk rocked and creaked as I climbed on. It would not have surprised me if the whole lot had collapsed.

Whenever we arrived at a new place, there was always a mad scramble to get the best places for your particular set-up. The engineers went after a portacabin near to where the two Chinooks were parked. I took what was one of the best rooms in the condemned building as the medical centre. Even so, there were huge holes in the walls and rubbish and dirt everywhere. I knew I would have no back-up on this trip as we were tucked away in the corner of the camp and instructed not to roam around. A few buildings away were the SAS guys. As usual, they kept themselves to themselves, coming over only when there was a need to communicate with someone or to steal a bit of kit. We all quickly fell in to the usual deployment routine, with everyone quietly getting on with their own particular jobs and tasks. I would always help out wherever possible, as thankfully I was only needed when there was an accident or illness. On this trip, my main responsibility would be that of field hygiene. Even though we were in hardened accommodation, it was in such a state that infection or infestation was a real possibility. Fortunately, there was only one occasion where someone found a rat in their kitbag. After that, all kitbags were kept off the floor!

Sorties came, and sorties went. About four days into the week, I was asked whether or not I would like to go on a deployment with the Boat Troop. This had been arranged without my knowledge as a thank you and farewell present from the Squadron. I jumped at the opportunity. The following day, I was kitted out in an all in one waterproof immersion suit and a life jacket. Walking out to the back of the Chinook I had to negotiate the large inflatable craft sitting inside the cabin. This would be going out the back of the aircraft – with me following it! I was really excited about the prospect. The flight out to where we would deploy took about 30 minutes. During the flight I was briefed by one of the SAS Boat Troop specialists. He told me that all I needed to do was to push the boat out of the back of the helicopter and just keep running. His last instruction was, "Try not to land on the boat as you'll probably kill yourself!"

The Chinook carried out a low pass over the location of the drop. Normal practice is for the helicopter to carry out a shallow dive towards the water, pulling up at about 40 – 50 feet above sea level. As the aircraft goes nose up, the inflatable craft is pushed out of the back, with the troops following. It would be interesting as the weather conditions were not as ideal as possible. Looking out of the side window, I could easily make out little white crests on the tops of the waves. It was about a Force 5. The Chinook banked into the turn that signified our final approach to the drop zone. The rear ramp was lowered and the cold damp air rushed into the cabin. "Ready." shouted the crewman at the ramp. The four of us, three guys from the SAS boat troop and myself, who were going out of the back, stood up to take our positions at the bow of the boat, two on either side. The boat would be pushed out backwards as the heavy out-board engine would drop faster than the lighter bow. As we pushed the boat out, we would be expected to continue running and follow it out of the helicopter. Any hesitation would mean that the boat could be several hundred metres away when you surfaced. Plus the fact that the other three team members would be a long way off too! The bell in the rear cabin of the Chinook rang once and the red light to the right hand side of the rear ramp came on.

"Red on. Stand by, stand by!" shouted the crewman. We pushed the bow of the boat toward the gaping hole at the rear of the helicopter. It did not move, as it was secured to the cabin floor by one thin nylon rope. Aware of the water below, I could only focus on how I was going to exit the aircraft and that I was determined that I would not pause after the boat had gone. The bell rang twice and the red light changed to green. At the same time as shouting "Green on, Go!" the forward loadmaster cut the rope at the bow of the boat. We lunged forward towards the gaping hole at the rear of this moving helicopter. All of a sudden the weight of the boat disappeared as it dropped off the back ramp and was caught in the slipstream and downdraft of the rotors. Without hesitation, I followed, falling about 40 feet into the cold, choppy sea. The fall took what felt like quite a few seconds, before I slammed into the water, disappearing under the surface for a short while. If I had fitted my immersion suit incorrectly, all the air inside could be pushed down the legs of the suit, causing me to float upside down in the water. If this were to happen, I would have a serious problem. Thankfully, I had managed to fit the suit properly and I felt myself quickly floating upwards.

Once on the surface, I looked around for the other three people who had jumped with me. Everyone was accounted for and we all tried to swim after the boat. Unfortunately, the current was too strong and the boat was being swept away from us, quicker than we could swim after it. Swimming in the immersion suit was really difficult as it was heavy and cumbersome and the loose material was causing too much drag. Eventually, the Chinook returned to winch one of the SAS guys from the sea and into the boat. Once on board, he sorted out the out board motor and rushed around collecting us all from the water. The plan was to go for a high-speed dash across the water and meet up with the Chinook on a regular basis. This would test the timekeeping and navigation skills of all on the exercise, as well as the boat handling skills of the SAS operators. Once everyone was on board, the first task took place. The boat was hurtling along the water and the Chinook flew in from behind. With the Loadmaster calling out the speed to the pilots, the Chinook matched the speed of the boat. Great skills and teamwork from the helicopter crew, as the pilots could not see the boat at all. The winch was lowered and I was nominated to be the first to be winched back into the helicopter. I placed the bright orange strop over my head and secured it in place under my arms. Once the signal was given, the Chinook rose about ten feet, lifting me clear from the boat. As the boat turned sharply away I thought that I would continue to be winched up. However, the crew had other ideas. The helicopter descended slowly until I was being trawled through the water. I looked up and saw a laughing crewman giving me the thumbs up sign. I replied with the two-fingered salute.

When they thought I had had enough, I gradually rose out of the water. Once about twenty feet clear of the water, I remained at that height as the helicopter lowered itself towards me. The strop had moved slightly during the 'trawling' session, and I was now being supported mainly by the lifejacket strap that passed between my legs. To say it was painful would be an understatement! The crewman could see that my eyes were bulging with the pain and he was almost crying with laughter as he pulled me into the cabin. After the pain had subsided, I jumped off the ramp back into the water. I was collected by a fast pass of the boat, where you 'punch' your arm through a hoop, which is held over the side of the boat. The momentum flicks you up into the boat and away you go. It was then my turn to watch others being winched away, although no one else got the trawling treatment.

However, we were soon surrounded by several small boats, some claiming to be from the French Coast Guard. Apparently, someone had seen us push the boat out of the back of the helicopter, without it slowing down, and then fly off into the distance. They had not seen it return to collect someone from the water. A report had been sent to the Coast Guard that there was a helicopter in trouble and the crew had 'evacuated', leaving it to fly off into the distance. A short explanation that this was a military exercise soon saw all the boats leaving us alone, although we were getting some funny looks. It was decided to abort the training due to the unnecessary attention that we were now getting. We drove our boat high up onto a nearby beach and called the Chinook back in to collect us. A short while later, with the Chinook hovering just over the beach, we manhandled the boat up the back ramp and climbed on board ourselves. Due to the downdraft of the rotors, and the fact that we were all wet, we were covered from head to toe in sand. Every which way we moved caused chafing of the skin, and we were all red raw by the time we got back to the camp. Standing naked under an outdoor fire hose in freezing October, washing away all the sand, is a memory that will remain with me for a long time! In fact, the whole opportunity will remain with me forever. I felt very honoured to have been allowed to take part. To my knowledge, there is no other RAF ground crew member who has done such a thing.

All too soon, my final deployment was over. The week passed and everything was loaded back into the two Chinooks. I had already made my decision to leave the RAF as I was being recommended for promotion, and this would mean that I would have to leave the Squadron. I didn't want to do that. I had also said that I would turn down the promotion if there were a guarantee that I could remain in post at RAF Odiham. I had been told that if I refused promotion, chances were that I would be posted in the same rank I currently held. I felt it was a no win situation for me. After being given the opportunity to work in the most highly specialized area of the RAF, I did not think that I would settle back into the normal routine of Medical Centre life too well. I was used to going away from home on a regular basis, living in poor accommodation and sometimes enduring hardship. I loved it! Not only that, it was a privilege for me to work with such professional people, not only my friends in the RAF Special Forces Flight, but also those I had made contact with in the SAS and the SBS. I felt that I had given a good account not only of myself, but also that of the RAF medical service. If the MoD would not allow me to stay where I was happy, it was time to go. I did not wish to become bitter and twisted. I haven't, and I look back on my time in the RAF with great pride and affection.

Once back at RAF Odiham, I began making preparations to leave. I handed over my secondary responsibilities and gradually, but reluctantly, handed over responsibility for primary duties to colleagues within the medical centre. My final major incident involved a civilian worker involved in the building of the new hangar complex on the south side of the airfield. He was apparently standing on top of a metal container unit, guiding a large sheet of steel into place somewhere in the construction. The chain holding the metal sheet to the crane gave way and caused the metal to fall and hit the worker. The call came through and off I dashed in the ambulance. On arrival the male was still on top of the container and in a great deal of pain. I got the ambulance parked next to the container and climbed up to where the patient was. My assessment was that he was seriously injured and would require treatment that could only be given by a doctor. Using the ambulance radio, I asked the Air Traffic Controller to contact the doctor and get them to meet me at the scene. While I was waiting for their arrival, I covered the man in a blanket and administered some entonox, pain relieving gas. I suspected that he had broken his pelvis. Whilst waiting with the man, I was thinking about how I was going to get him down from the top of the container. If his pelvis was broken, it would put him in a lot more pain getting him down. The doctor arrived fairly quickly and gave me permission to give a pethidine injection. This took effect quite quickly and the man began to settle. I still had the problem of getting him down though. Nearby was a JCB digger, complete with front bucket. I got the ambulance driver to take one of the canvas stretchers from the back of the ambulance and see if it would fit in the bucket. Fortunately it did. I had the stretcher passed up to me, as well as one of the aeromedical stretcher harnesses. This harness was designed to fit over the general-purpose military canvass stretcher and hold the patient to the stretcher from five separate points. I was well practiced in the fitting of the harness and soon had everything ready to get the patient securely strapped in. The driver climbed up and helped me lift the patient into the stretcher. I then strapped him in securely and called the JCB over to where we were. The JCB driver raised the bucket and inched his way towards us. Once level, the ambulance driver and I lifted the stretcher into the bucket. The patient was as comfortable as could be expected but was still in extreme pain. I stood on the edge of the bucket, to prevent the stretcher from falling out, and very slowly, the JCB backed away from the container. Once a few feet away from the container, the bucket was slowly lowered. All the time the patient continued to let me know that he was in pain. Once at ground level, we transferred him to the back of our ambulance and took him off to the medical centre. We couldn't go straight to hospital, as that would have left the airfield without ambulance cover and that would have stopped all flying. As we arrived back at the medical centre, I saw that a civilian ambulance was already there waiting for us. One of the other medics had called for them, knowing that our ambulance wouldn't be able to leave. The patient was transferred and whisked of to the local hospital at Basingstoke. I later found out that he had, indeed, fractured his pelvis. It could have been a lot worse though!

Finally, my last day in the RAF came – 6 December 1992. I handed over my identification card and walked out through the main gate of RAF Odiham for the last time as an airman. It was the right thing to do. I was extremely sad at leaving, but also immensely proud of not only my achievements, but also the achievements of those with whom I had had the honour to serve. To this day, I look back with satisfaction at my little contribution whilst serving my country. Without doubt though, my career highlight was as the medic on the Royal Air Force Special Forces Flight. A little known, but highly respected, specialized and thoroughly professional force, whose motto is quite apt: Per diem, per noctem - By day and by night.

Gentlemen, the honour was mine.

I bring this prayer to You, Lord
For You alone can give
What one cannot demand from oneself.
Give me, Lord, what you have left over,
Give me what no-one ever asks You for.
I don't ask You for rest,
Or quiet,
Whether of soul or body;
I don't ask You for wealth,
Nor for success, nor even health perhaps.
That sort of thing You get asked for so much
That You can't have any of it left.
Give me, Lord, what you have left over,
Give me what no-one wants from you.
I want insecurity, strife,
And I want You to give me these
Once and for all.
So that I can be sure of having them always,
Since I shall not always have the courage
To ask You for them.
Give me, Lord, what You have left over,
Give me what others want nothing to do with.
But give me courage too,
And strength and faith;
For You alone can give
What one cannot demand from oneself.

Found in the uniform of Lt. Andre Zirnheld, SAS.
Killed in battle July 26, 1941.

Lightning Source UK Ltd.
Milton Keynes UK
20 October 2009

145193UK00002B/130/P